Sports in America
1980–1989
SECOND EDITION

MICHAEL TEITELBAUM

SERIES FOREWORD BY
LARRY KEITH

CHELSEA HOUSE
PUBLISHERS
An imprint of Infobase Publishing

1980–1989, Second Edition
Sports in America

Copyright © 2010, 2004 Michael Teitelbaum
Foreword copyright © 2010 Larry Keith

Chelsea House
An imprint of Infobase Publishing
132 West 31st Street
New York NY 10001

Library of Congress Cataloging-in-Publication Data

Teitelbaum, Michael.
  Sports in America, 1980-1989 / Michael Teitelbaum. — 2nd ed.
    p. cm.
  Includes bibliographical references and index.
  ISBN-13: 978-1-60413-455-1 (hardcover)
  ISBN-10: 1-60413-455-0 (hardcover)
  1. Sports—United States—History—20th century. I. Title.

  GV583.T45 2010
  796.0973'09048—dc22

                    2010002803

Chelsea House books are available at special discounts when purchased in bulk quantities for businesses, associations, institutions, or sales promotions. Please call our Special Sales Department in New York at (212) 967-8800 or (800) 322-8755.

You can find Chelsea House on the World Wide Web at http://www.chelseahouse.com

Produced by the Shoreline Publishing Group LLC
President/Editorial Director: James Buckley Jr.
Contributing Editors: Jim Gigliotti, Beth Adelman
Text design and composition by Thomas Carling, carlingdesign.com
Index by Nanette Cardon, IRIS

Photo credits: AP/Wide World: 15, 20, 29, 47 (2), 48, 51, 56, 57, 62, 64, 65, 68, 69, 70 (left), 72, 75, 77, 78, 81, 88; Corbis: 7, 9, 13, 19, 27, 39, 89; Getty Images: 3, 8, 11, 14, 16, 22, 23, 25, 32, 35, 36, 41, 43, 45, 52, 55, 59, 60, 67, 70 (right), 83, 87; Sports icons by Bob Eckstein.

Cover printed by Bang Printing, Brainerd, MN
Book printed and bound by Bang Printing, Brainerd, MN
Date printed: July 2010

Printed in the United States of America.

10 9 8 7 6 5 4 3 2 1

This book is printed on acid-free paper.

CONTENTS

Walter Payton (page 45)

FOREWORD

BY LARRY KEITH

WHEN THE EDITORS OF SPORTS IN AMERICA invited me to write the foreword to this important historical series I recalled my experience in the 1980s as the adjunct professor for a new sports journalism course in the graduate school of Columbia University. Before granting their approval, the faculty at that prestigious Ivy League institution asked, Do sports matter? Are they relevant? Are they more than just fun and games?

The answer—an emphatic yes—is even more appropriate today than it was then. As an integral part of American society, sports provide insights to our history and culture and, for better or worse, help define who we are.

Sports In America is much more than a compilation of names, dates, and facts. Each volume chronicles accomplishments and expansions of the possible. Not just in the physical ability to perform, but in the ability to create goals and determine methods to achieve them. In this way, sports, the sweaty offspring of recreation and competition, resemble any other field of endeavor. I certainly wouldn't equate the race for a gold medal with the race to the moon, but the building blocks are the same: the intelligent application of talent, determination, research, practice, and hard work to a meaningful objective.

Sports matter because they show us in high definition. They communicate examples of determination, courage, and skill. They often embody a heroic human-interest story, overcoming poverty, injustice, injury, or disease. The phrase, "Sports is a microcosm of life," could also read "Life is a microcosm of sport."

Consider racial issues. When Jackie Robinson of the Brooklyn Dodgers broke through major league baseball's "color barrier" in 1947, the significance extended beyond the national pastime. Precisely because baseball was the national pastime, this epochal event reverberated throughout every part of American society.

To be sure, black stars from individual sports had preceded him (notably Joe Louis in boxing and Jesse Owens in track), and others would follow (Arthur Ashe in tennis and Tiger Woods in golf), but Robinson stood out as an important member of a team. He wasn't just playing with the Dodgers, he was traveling with them, living with them. He was a black member of a white athletic family. The benefits of integration could be appreciated far beyond the borough of Brooklyn. In 1997, Major League Baseball retired his "42" jersey number.

Sports have always been a laboratory for social awareness and change. Robinson integrated big league box scores eight years before the U.S. Supreme Court ordered the integration of public schools. The Paralympics (1960) and Special Olympics (1968) easily predate the Americans with Disabilities Act (1990). The mainstreaming of disabled athletes was especially apparent in 2007 when double amputee Jessica Long, 15, won the AAU Sullivan Award as America's top amateur. Women's official debut in the Olympic Games, though limited to swimming, occurred in 1912, seven years before they got the right to vote. So even if these sports were tardy in opening their doors, in another way, they were ahead of their times. And if it was necessary to break down some of those doors—Title IX support for female college athletes comes to mind—so be it. Basketball star Candace Parker won't let anyone keep her from the hoop.

Another area of importance, particularly as it affects young people, is substance abuse. High school, college, and professional teams all oppose the illegal use of drugs, tobacco, and alcohol. In most venues, testing is mandatory, and tolerance is zero. The confirmed use of performance enhancing drugs has damaged the reputations of such superstar athletes as Olympic sprinters Ben Johnson and Marion Jones, cyclist Floyd Landis, and baseball sluggers Manny Ramirez and Alex Rodriguez. Some athletes have lost their careers, or even their lives, to substance abuse. Conversely, other athletes have used their fame to caution young people about submitting to peer pressure or making poor choices.

Fans care about sports and sports personalities because they provide entertainment and self-identify—too often at a loss of priorities. One reason sports have flourished in this country is their support from governmental bodies. When a city council votes to help underwrite the cost of a sports facility or give financial advantages to the owners of a team, it affects the pocketbook of every taxpayer, not to mention the local ecosystem. When high schools and colleges allocate significant resources to athletics, administrators believe they are serving the greater good, but at what cost? Decisions with implications beyond the sports page merit everyone's attention.

In World War II, our country's sporting passion inspired President Franklin Roosevelt to declare that professional games should not be cancelled. He felt the benefits to the national psyche outweighed the risk of gathering large crowds at central locations. In 2001, another generation of Americans also continued to attend large-scale sports events because, to do otherwise, would "let the terrorists win." Being there, being a fan, yelling your lungs out, cheering victory and bemoaning defeat, is a cleansing, even therapeutic exercise. The security check at the gate is just part of the price of stepping inside. Even before there was a 9/11, there was a bloody terrorist assault at the Munich Olympic Games in 1972.

The popular notion "Sports build character" has been better expressed "Sports reveal character." We've witnessed too many coaches and athletes break rules of fair play and good conduct. The convictions of NBA referee Tim Donaghy for gambling and NFL quarterback Michael Vick for operating a dog-fighting ring are startling recent examples. We've even seen violence and cheating in youth sports, often by parents of a (supposed) future superstar. We've watched (at a safe distance) fans "celebrate" championships with destructive behavior. I would argue, however, that these flaws are the exception, not the rule, that the good of sports far outweighs the bad, that many of life's success stories took root on an athletic field.

Any serious examination of sports leads to the question of athletes as standards for conduct. Professional basketball star Charles Barkley created quite a stir in 1993 when he used a Nike shoe commercial to declare, "I am not paid to be a role model." The knee-jerk response argued, "Of course you are, because kids look up to you," but Barkley was right to raise the issue. He was saying that, in making lifestyle choices in language and behavior, young people should look elsewhere for role models, ideally to responsible parents or guardians.

The fact remains, however, that athletes occupy an exalted place in our society, especially when they are magnified in the mass media, sports talk radio, and the blogosphere. The athletes we venerate can be as young as a high school basketball player or as old as a Hall of Famer. (They can even be dead, as Babe Ruth's commercial longevity attests.) They are honored and coddled in a way few mortals are. Regrettably, we can be quick to excuse their excesses and ignore their indulgences. They influence the way we live and think: Ted Williams inspired patriotism as a wartime fighter pilot; Muhammad Ali's opposition to the Vietnam War on religious grounds, validated by the Supreme Court, encouraged the peace movement; Magic Johnson's contraction of the HIV/AIDs virus brought better understanding to a little-understood disease. No wonder we elect them—track stars, football coaches, baseball pitchers—to represent us in Washington. Meanwhile, television networks pay huge sums to sports leagues so their teams can pay fortunes for their services.

Indeed, it has always been this way. If we, as a nation, love sports, then we, quite naturally, will love the men and women who play them best. In return, they provide entertainment, release and inspiration. From the beginning of the 20th century until now, Sports In America is their story-and ours.

Larry Keith is the former Assistant Managing Editor of Sports Illustrated. *He created the editorial concept for* SI Kids *and was the editor of the official Olympic programs in 1996, 2000 and 2002. He is a former adjunct professor of Sports Journalism at Columbia University and is a member of the North Carolina Journalism Hall of Fame.*

INTRODUCTION
1980–1989

IT WAS A DECADE OF EXCESS. IT WAS a time of a new "morning in America," as incoming President Ronald Reagan (1911-2004) called it after his election in 1980. Reagan served as President during some of the most financially prosperous years in American history.

The stock market soared. Peace symbols from the 1960s and 1970s were traded in for Mercedes-Benz logos, and tie-dyed T-shirts were replaced by three-piece suits. Business schools, investment banks, and Wall Street law firms were filled with a new breed of achievers, called yuppies (young urban professionals), who were making money—and lots of it.

As the money poured in, many people succumbed to the lure of illegal drugs. Cocaine use soared, not just among the desperate poor, who were devastated by the scourge of crack-cocaine, but also among those well-off enough to afford the excess. The world of sports was by no means immune to either the draw of big money or the temptations of drugs—both mind-altering substances, such as cocaine, and performance-enhancing drugs, such as steroids.

There were several unfortunate examples of this. In 1986, college basketball superstar Len Bias, a young man destined for NBA stardom, died suddenly from cocaine use, just days after being drafted by the Boston Celtics. One of baseball's great pitchers, Dwight Gooden (b.1964) was suspended for cocaine use, just one year after leading the New York Mets to a World Series win in 1986 and just two years after a Cy Young Award-winning season. In and out of rehab for the next few years, the player known as "Doc" would never again be the pitcher he was. At the 1988 Summer Olympics in Seoul, South Korea, Canadian sprinter Ben Johnson was sent home in disgrace and stripped of his world-record gold medal after testing positive for performance-enhancing steroids.

The decade in sports began with a "miracle" (see page 10) and ended with a natural disaster (see page 86).

As American citizens were held hostage in Iran, the Soviet Union invaded Afghanistan, and the cold war raged, a group of unknown college hockey players staged one of the greatest upsets in sports history, the so-called Miracle on Ice, at the 1980 Winter Olympic Games in Lake Placid, New York. It gave a boost to a nation that was burdened with double-

The Road to Washington   *Ronald Reagan and his wife, Nancy, wave to supporters at the Republican National Convention in July of 1980. Four months later, Reagan was elected the 40th President of the United States.*

digit inflation, declining productivity, and a diminished place on the world stage.

The decade drew to a shattering close as an earthquake struck San Francisco just moments before the start of game three of the 1989 World Series in Candlestick Park. In an instant, players' chief concerns switched from the best game strategies to the safety of family members in the trembling stadium. Images of play-

1980-
1989

ers hugging their wives and carrying their children from the field reminded fans that no matter how important sports are—even the World Series—they are after all, just games. This was life—real, unstoppable, and potentially deadly. The Series was an afterthought in the wake of this reminder of the raw power of nature.

All three Summer Olympics in the 1980s were tainted by outside issues such as politics, boycotts, and drug use. The line between sports and politics blurred as the United States boycotted the 1980 Summer Olympic Games in Moscow as a response to the Soviet Union's invasion of Afghanistan a year earlier. The Soviets returned the favor four years later, boycotting the 1984 Olympics in Los Angeles.

The role of business and money in sports had been growing decade by decade and reached new heights in the 1980s. Sneaker endorsements and multi-million dollar player contracts pushed the economics of sports to stratospheric levels, unthinkable a few years earlier. If baseball star Bobby Bonilla was worth $29 million, what would legendary heroes such as Mickey Mantle (1931–1995) or Ted Williams (1918–2002) be worth in the free-agent market had they been in their prime in the 1980s? If basketball player Moses Malone could be paid $13.2 million, what would 11-time champion Bill Russell (b.1934) or record-setting scorer Wilt Chamberlain (1936–1999) have been worth if they played in the 1980s?

Shaken Spectators *A major earthquake struck the San Francisco Bay Area shortly before the Giants and Athletics were to play Game 3 of the World Series.*

Television money also gained a larger influence over sports. For the first time, most major sports team owners took in more money from selling television rights than from selling tickets to fans. As the money flowed in, players demanded that more of it flow into their pockets. Both baseball and football experienced prolonged player strikes as the battle for dollars supplanted the quest for victories.

Early in the decade, AIDS, a deadly new disease, emerged, at first believed to be limited to certain groups, but soon spreading to the wider population. Movie idol Rock Hudson's death from AIDS in 1985 put a familiar face on the previously shadowy disease, and placed its sadness in the front of the American mind. A few years later, one of the 1980s' greatest athletes, Los Angeles Lakers basketball superstar Magic Johnson (b.1959), announced that he was HIV-positive (HIV is the virus that leads to AIDS).

But, as is always the case, the world of sports in the 1980s was not exclusively filled with bad news. The decade saw Wayne Gretzky (b.1961) re-write the National Hockey League (NHL) record book.

The National Basketball Association (NBA), which started the decade with its popularity at an all-time low, combined the play of Johnson and Larry Bird (b.1956) with the business and marketing brilliance of its new commissioner, David Stern (b.1942), to rocket its way to new heights of success.

Pete Rose (b.1941) became baseball's all-time hits leader, although by decade's end he was banned for life from the game because of allegations that he had bet on

Court Battles *Magic Johnson (32) and the Los Angeles Lakers often went head-to-head with Larry Bird and the Boston Celtics for the NBA title in the 1980s.*

baseball. Kareem Abdul-Jabbar (b.1947) became the NBA's all-time leading scorer, Walter Payton (1954–1999) became the leading rusher in the history of the National Football League (NFL), and Joan Benoit Samuelson (b.1957) proved that women could run Olympic marathons—in many cases faster than men.

The blending of sports and business was completed during the 1980s, and the intrusion of real-life issues such as drug abuse could not be kept from locker rooms. But from the glistening miracle in Lake Placid to the rumbling stands of Candlestick, many teams and individuals reminded us that despite the real world's rude intrusion into our beloved games, America's obsession with sports would only continue to grow.

1980

The Miracle on Ice

As the final seconds ticked down in the United States' improbable 4–3 victory over the Soviet Union in the semifinals of the Olympic hockey competition in Lake Placid, New York, television announcer Al Michaels delivered the words that still reverberate more than a quarter of a century later: "Do you believe in miracles? Yes!"

The United States' victory over the Soviets was indeed a miracle by sports standards. The 1980 U.S. Olympic hockey team was made up of young college and minor league players who had never played together before the Olympic team was chosen. The national team from the Soviet Union was a powerhouse that had been playing together as a unit for many years. That squad defeated the United States team 10–3 in an exhibition game a few weeks before the Olympics, and was considered by many experts to be the best hockey team in the world.

Add to that the politically charged atmosphere of the Cold War between the United States and the Soviet Union, and the stage was set for one of the greatest upsets in sports history.

To reach the medal round, head coach Herb Brooks' American squad tied the talented team from Sweden in its opening game, then beat perennially powerful Czechoslovakia 7–3 en route to four wins and a tie in the opening round.

On February 22—which just happened to be George Washington's birthday—the United States team faced off against the Soviet Union. The 10,000 fans at the Olympic Field House screamed and chanted "USA! USA!" as an electric atmosphere filled the building. Before the game, Brooks told his team, "You were born to be players. You were meant to be here. This moment is yours."

The Soviet Union jumped out to an early 1–0 lead. But the pesky, scrappy United States team tied it. The Soviets went back up 2–1, but as the clock ran down near the end of the first period, a rebound goal by American Mark Johnson tied the contest once again.

Hard checking by the American skaters and gutsy goaltending by United States goalie Jim Craig kept the game close. The Soviets never managed to extend their lead to more than one goal, and they left the ice at the end of the second period leading 3–2.

Miracles Do Happen *Jubilant U.S. hockey players celebrate their Olympic semifinal victory over the Soviet Union.*

Johnson scored his second goal of the game—this one on a power play, while the Soviets were playing one man short—in the third period, tying the game and raising the decibel level of the crowd another notch. Halfway through the final period, United States captain Mike Eruzione found the net with a 30-foot slapshot that gave the Americans their first lead of the game.

Pandemonium broke loose in the crowd, and the chanting of "USA! USA!" continued non-stop. Now it was up to Craig and the United States' defense to hold the mighty Soviets scoreless.

Checking and swarming their opponents, the American team managed to prevent the Soviets from scoring.

The United States team had done the impossible. They had beaten the best. Two days later, in the almost anticlimactic gold medal game, the United States beat Finland 4–2 to capture the gold. The outpouring of patriotism around the United States following the victory was as great as any since the end of World War II.

1980

Heiden's Golden Games

Over the course of nine days in February, American speed skater Eric Heiden (b.1958) did what no other Olympic athlete had ever done before at either the Winter or Summer Games—he won five individual gold medals in one Olympics. The 21-year-old speed skater from Madison, Wisconsin, dominated every event in which he participated.

Although at the time his astounding performance was somewhat overshadowed by the emotional victory of the United States hockey team, time has not diminished Heiden's accomplishment.

Heiden took part in five speed skating events, and won the gold medal in all five. He broke the Olympic record in winning the speed skating competitions at 500, 1,000, 1,500, 5,000, and 10,000 meters. He completed his gold-medal sweep—the drive for five, as it was called at the time—in the 10,000-meter race on February 23. Heiden had spent the previous day watching the United States upset the Soviets in hockey. Then he went out and smashed the existing world record in the 10,000 by more than six seconds.

"He gave the most dominant performance in the history of mankind in an Olympic competition," television announcer Keith Jackson said.

Boycott

Nowhere did the worlds of politics and sports clash more blatantly than in the United States' boycott of the 1980 Summer Olympic Games in Moscow. In December of 1979, the Soviet Union invaded neighboring Afghanistan, and U.S. President Jimmy Carter called for a boycott of the Games to protest the invasion.

On April 12, the United States Olympic Committee (USOC) voted to endorse Carter's call for a boycott. The vote was taken at a meeting in Colorado Springs attended by hundreds of athletes, plus sports and business leaders. Hours of angry debate followed, along with an appeal from Vice President Walter Mondale for everyone to support the boycott.

American athletes were devastated. They had trained for years, some had been preparing for the Games their entire lives and now, through no fault of their

---

Eric Heiden's 1980 Olympics Speed Skating Results

500 meters	38.03 seconds	Olympic Record	Gold Medal
1,000 meters	1 minute, 15.18 seconds	Olympic Record	Gold Medal
1,500 meters	1 minute, 55.44 seconds	Olympic Record	Gold Medal
5,000 meters	7 minutes, 02.29 seconds	Olympic Record	Gold Medal
10,000 meters	14 minutes, 28.13 seconds	World Record	Gold Medal

The Girls Are Alright

In 1932, at the Winter Olympics in Lake Placid, New York, 21 female athletes competed in the Games. Less than half a century later, at the 1980 Winter Olympics, also at Lake Placid, 233 women competed. Figure skater Linda Fratianne was the American star, winning a silver medal in Ladies Singles.

It wasn't only at the Olympics, though, that female athletes made headlines in 1980:

- In January, Mary Decker turned in the first sub-four-and-a-half-minute mile. Decker ran the mile in 4 minutes and 21.68 seconds in Auckland, New Zealand.

- In October, Norway's Grete Waitz was the women's winner in the New York City Marathon for the third year in a row. She completed the 26-plus miles in 2 hours, 25 minutes, and 41 seconds.

- The charter class of the International Women's Sports Hall of Fame included Babe Didrikson (golf, track), Althea Gibson (tennis), Janet Guthrie (auto racing), and Billie Jean King (tennis).

Linda Fratianne

own, they would be denied the chance to compete at the Olympic level.

Twenty-five members of the 1980 United States Olympic team who were slated to go to Moscow sued the USOC. They claimed the USOC did not have the power to decide not to enter an American team in the Olympics. They also claimed the law stated that any decision to not participate in an Olympic games had to be "sports-related." The court rejected all of their claims. The boycott stood.

More than 60 other countries joined the United States in the boycott and did not send teams to Moscow.

In retaliation for the U.S.-led boycott, the Soviet Union refused to send a team to the Olympic Games in Los Angeles, California, in the summer of 1984 (see page 46).

It's Showtime!

In the spring of 1979, Earvin "Magic" Johnson's Michigan State University team beat Larry Bird's Indiana State University team for the National Collegiate Athletic Association (NCAA) basketball championship. That fall, both players entered the NBA as promising rookies for the 1979–80 season.

By the end of the 1980s, the rivalry between the two players dominated and re-defined professional basketball, bringing the NBA to new heights of popularity. Johnson's Los Angeles Lakers won five NBA championships during the decade, and Bird's Boston Celtics captured three NBA titles. The two teams met three times in the NBA Finals (1983–84, 1984–85 and 1986–87) during the Magic-Bird years.

No Contest *Muhammad Ali (facing camera) fought Larry Holmes, but by this point in their careers, Ali's former sparring partner was the better boxer.*

Johnson's arrival in Los Angeles teamed him with center Kareem Abdul-Jabbar, creating a brand of basketball that came to be known as "Showtime."

At 6-foot-9, Johnson was the tallest point guard in NBA history. He ran the offense, scoring and passing. At a time in the league when individual performances dominated, Johnson got all his teammates involved in the offense, creating a true team effort.

Because of his height, speed and strength, Johnson could play forward or center, as well as guard. He demonstrated his versatility in game six of the NBA Finals in 1980, when the Lakers met the Philadelphia 76ers on May 16.

Jabbar sprained his ankle in game five of the finals. The Lakers led the series three games to two, but they would have to play game six in Philadelphia without their all-star center.

Johnson, a rookie who had played all season at point guard, filled in for Jabbar at center. He scored 42 points, pulled down 15 rebounds, and dished out seven assists, leading the Lakers to a 123–107 victory to take the NBA title. Many consider it to be his finest game as a pro, stepping up when his team needed him most.

On thing was for certain: Showtime had arrived!

Marathon Tennis Match

In a match that lasted an astounding three hours and 53 minutes, 24-year-old Bjorn Borg (b.1956) of Sweden won his fifth consecutive Wimbledon singles tennis championship on July 5. His opponent in this titanic struggle was 21-year-old American John McEnroe (b.1959), who went on to win three of the next four Wimbledon singles titles.

Borg lost the first set 1–6, then came back to take the second 7–5. He grabbed the lead, winning the third set 6–3. The intense fourth set, which could have given Borg the title, ended with a marathon 34-point tiebreaker. McEnroe survived three match points and eventually won the tie-breaker 18–16, giving Borg a 6–7 defeat.

In the fifth and final set, Borg's serve overpowered McEnroe, giving the Swede 19 straight points and an 8–6 win. The victory represented Borg's fifth straight Wimbledon title and his 35th consecutive victory in a Wimbledon match—a tournament record.

Holmes Stops Ali

Muhammad Ali (b.1942) was a three-time heavyweight boxing champion of the world, but he never had much of a chance in his bid for a fourth crown, falling to Larry Holmes (b.1949) in a one-sided fight in Las Vegas, Nevada, on October 2.

Holmes, who at one time had been a sparring partner of Ali's and who counted the former champ among his personal heroes, was the younger, faster, and stronger fighter, and Ali was in trouble from the start. Holmes danced and punched, showing the type of power and speed that were Ali's trademarks in his prime. Ali gamely hung on through 10 rounds, but at that point, the referee stopped the fight, and Holmes retained his title.

For Ali, it was clear his storied career was nearing its end. In 1960, Ali had won the gold medal at the Olympics. In 1964, at the age of 22, he shocked the world by beating heavily favored Sonny Liston to capture the heavyweight championship. In 1967, when he refused to be drafted into the military because of his religious beliefs, the title was taken away from him. Then, in 1974, the 32-year-old Ali stunned the world again by beating the previously invincible George Foreman (b.1949) to capture the heavyweight title for a second time.

In 1978, Olympic gold medalist Leon Spinks beat Ali to take his title. Six months later, Ali won the rematch to grab the championship for a third time. After two

Victory at Last! *Bjorn Borg won his fifth consecutive men's singles championship at Wimbledon, but it wasn't easy. He needed five sets to beat up-and-coming John McEnroe in an epic struggle.*

1980

years in retirement, the Champ tried for one more comeback against Holmes, but was totally overmatched.

Ali would fight just one more time in his career, but was beaten by Trevor Berbick in a non-title fight in the Bahamas in 1981 (see page 22).

"No Mas" for Duran

They could not have been more different in personality or boxing style. Welterweight champion Sugar Ray Leonard (b.1956) was a fast-moving, quick-legged dancer in the ring. He borrowed his boxing style and moves from Muhammad Ali and from his namesake, Sugar Ray Robinson, a welterweight and middleweight champion in the 1940s and 1950s. Leonard's good looks and charming personality captured a legion of fans, and

in many ways he filled the vacuum left by Ali's retirement. "I studied Ali, I studied Sugar Ray Robinson, I watched them display showmanship, personality, and charisma," Leonard said in an interview on *ABC's Wide World of Sports*. "I wanted to transcend the sport. I wanted to be considered not just a fighter or a champion, but someone special."

Roberto Duran (b.1951), on the other hand, was a powerful puncher who destroyed opponents with his "hands of stone." Duran was already a great lightweight champion when he fought Leonard for the welterweight title, and he had much more experience. Their meeting on June 20, in Montreal, Canada, was perhaps the most eagerly anticipated non-heavyweight fight in history.

Duran was famous for his psychological intimidation. When he ran into

Other Milestones of 1980

✔ On February 29, hockey great Gordie Howe (b.1928) scored his record 800th regular-season NHL goal, at the age of 51. Howe, playing for the Hartford Whalers, scored one more time before retiring at the end of the season.

✔ Nineteen-year-old NHL rookie Wayne Gretzky won the first of his eight consecutive Most Valuable Player awards (also called the Hart Trophy). Gretzky became the youngest player ever to receive this honor.

Jack Nicklaus

✔ George Brett came closer to batting .400 than anyone else in Major League Baseball since Ted Williams did it in 1941. Brett stayed right near the .400 mark until late September, and ended the season with a .390 average.

✔ Jack Nicklaus won the U.S. Open and the PGA Championship (left) to up his record number of men's major golf titles to 17. Nicklaus eventually won one more major in his storied career, at the 1986 Masters (see page 60).

Leonard on the street shortly before the fight, Duran made rude gestures, threats and insults to Leonard and his wife.

By the time the fight began, Leonard's trainer, Angelo Dundee—who had also trained Ali—recalled that Leonard was so angry at Duran about the insults that he was ready to go after him as if in a street brawl. Dundee reminded Leonard that his skills were superior and that he should outbox Duran, as they had planned.

But Leonard came out brawling, trying to beat Duran at his own game. After a 15-round slugfest, Duran won a unanimous decision, taking the welterweight title away from Leonard. A rematch was quickly scheduled.

In an interview with ABC Sports, Dundee explained Leonard's mind-set going into the second fight. "He was embarrassed that he lost the first fight," Dundee said. "He realized what he was supposed to do the first time. And the first time, he was supposed to box. Ray was a premier boxer. What beats Duran, I knew, was a premier boxer."

In the rematch on November 25 at the New Orleans Superdome, Leonard stuck to the plan, outboxing and outdancing Duran for seven rounds, controlling the fight from the outset.

Then, in the eighth round, Duran threw up his hands and uttered the now-famous phrase, "No mas, no mas," which is Spanish for "No more." He quit the fight, claiming that he had stomach cramps, and Leonard regained his title.

Many at the fight said Duran appeared to lose heart, baffled by Leonard's shuffling feet and rapid-fire jabs. On that day, the skillful boxer beat the hands of stone.

1981

Wild Card Winner

The Oakland Raiders won the NFL championship by easily dispatching the Philadelphia Eagles 27–10 in Super Bowl XV at the Louisiana Superdome in New Orleans on January 25. It was the Raiders' second league title in five seasons; the Eagles were playing in the Super Bowl for the first time.

Oakland quarterback Jim Plunkett completed 13 of 21 passes for 261 yards and three touchdowns and was named the game's most valuable player. Plunkett came a long way from the beginning of the season, when he was on the Raiders' bench—a spot with which he was quite familiar.

Plunkett won the Heisman Trophy—college football's highest honor—in 1970. He was the No. 1 overall pick (by the New England Patriots) in the 1971 NFL Draft, and became an immediate starter. But his career never really took off as expected, and he was traded to the San Francisco 49ers in 1976. He joined Oakland in 1978, but had been a rarely used backup during his first two years with the Raiders.

In the fifth game of the season, Raiders starting quarterback Dan Pastorini was injured. Plunkett took over and finished the season, leading Oakland to an 11–5 record and the wild-card spot in the playoffs. (The wild-card spot goes to the second-place team in the conference with the best record; that team gets to join the division winners in the playoffs.)

In the postseason, Plunkett led the Raiders to victories over the Houston Oilers, Cleveland Browns and San Diego Chargers, leading the team to its third Super Bowl. Oakland lost Super Bowl II to the Green Bay Packers in the 1967 season, and beat the Minnesota Vikings in Super Bowl XI in the 1976 season.

Plunkett took control of Super Bowl XV right from the start. He threw three touchdown passes. The first was a two-yard toss to Cliff Branch in the first quarter. Then, just minutes later, Plunkett tossed a pass to running back Kenny King, which turned into an 80-yard score—the longest pass play in Super Bowl history. Plunkett's final touchdown pass was a 29-yarder to Branch in the third quarter.

Linebacker Rod Martin intercepted three Eagles' passes as the Oakland defense played tough. The Eagles did not reach the end zone until they trailed 24–3 in the fourth quarter.

Strike Two *Baseball's second strike was the first to stop play in the middle of the season (see page 21).*

Two for Every One

Wayne Gretzky's journey to re-write the NHL record books continued in his sophomore season, when Gretzky became the first player in the history of the league to average two points per game. His 1981 total was 164 points (goals plus assists) over an 82-game season. He had 55 goals and a record 109 assists.

These were just among the first of the mind-boggling statistics Gretzky posted during his NHL career. From the moment he set foot on the ice, he was the best passer and the best scorer in NHL history. In 1981 he captured his second league MVP award, but the best was yet to come.

Gretzky would go on to play through the 1998–99 season and finish with a host of league records, including most points (2,458), most goals (803), and most assists (1,655). His league scoring championship in 1980–81 was his first of a record nine scoring titles in his career.

Gretzky won the Hart Memorial Trophy as the league's MVP a record nine times, too.

1981

Hoosiers Win

At the NCAA basketball championship game on March 20, the University of North Carolina jumped out to an 8–2 lead over Indiana University, and later led by a score of 16–8. But Indiana's Randy Wittman helped close the gap, and his team led 27–26 at halftime.

As the game resumed in the second half, Indiana guard Isiah Thomas (b.1961) singlehandedly put the contest away.

During one seven-minute stretch at the beginning of the second half, the 6-foot-1 sophomore took over, leading Indiana to a 63–50 victory. He scored 10 of his game-high 23 points, consistently fed his teammates the ball, and pulled off key steals anytime it appeared that North Carolina was poised to get back into the game.

Earlier that same day, President Ronald Reagan was shot in an assassination attempt. It looked as if the game would be postponed. But when it became clear that the President was out of danger, the game proceeded. Still, a dark mood hung over the arena, dampening the usual frantic championship atmosphere.

The King of Daytona

Richard Petty's (b.1937) father, Lee Petty, began racing even before there was a National Association for Stock Car Automobile Racing (NASCAR, which began in 1949). And Richard slipped behind the wheel himself in 1958, beginning an unparalleled 34-year-career as a race car driver. His record 200 wins may never be surpassed, and his record of seven driving championships has been equaled only once (by the late, great Dale Earnhardt). Petty's nickname, appropriately enough, was "the King."

The Daytona 500 is the biggest, most well-known stock car race of the season. In the first Daytona 500, in 1959, Richard Petty ran into engine trouble and had to leave the race. His father ended up winning that day. Richard won his first Daytona 500 race in 1964.

He opened the 1981 racing season with his record seventh and final victory at the Daytona 500 on February 15. He averaged 169.651 miles per hour in his Buick over the course of the race. Petty's seven victories at Daytona came in 1964, 1966, 1971, 1973, 1974, 1979, and 1981. Petty retired from racing in 1992.

The King *Richard Petty's trademarks included his hat, dark glasses, and engaging grin—plus a record 200 career NASCAR victories. Seven of those wins came at the prestigious Daytona 500.*

Lewis Jumps to a Record

At the time, it was a huge achievement. Carl Lewis (b.1961), an extremely talented sophomore at the University of Houston, broke the world indoor long jump record in a meet on February 20. In retrospect, it was the first baby step for a man who would redefine the sport of track and field, picking up 10 medals in four Olympics—nine of those gold—over the next 16 years.

Lewis came into the Southwest Conference Indoor Track and Field Championship at Fort Worth, Texas, that February day as the NCAA champion in both the indoor and outdoor long jump.

The tall, 19-year-old from Birmingham, Alabama, broke the previous indoor record of 27 feet, 6 inches, set by Larry Myricks of Mississippi State in 1980. Lewis' personal best in the indoor long jump had been 27 feet, 4 inches. But this day he shattered both his own mark and the world record with a jump of 27 feet, 10.25 inches. To top off his record-breaking day, Lewis also won the 60-yard sprint, posting a time of 6.06 seconds—the third fastest time in history!

Strike Out!

Baseball, like all professional sports, is a diversion. For the fans, the games are a small break from the realities of life. But on June 12, the harsh reality of baseball as a business intruded, as the players went out on strike, stopping play and jeopardizing the season.

This was not the first baseball strike, nor would it be the last. On April 1, 1972,

---

Carl Lewis:
The Best Ever

The 1984 Olympics were not supposed to be Carl Lewis' first, but the United States team boycotted the Games in 1980 (see page 12), so the track and field star had to wait four years. At the 1984 Games in Los Angeles, he won four gold medals. Some athletes might have stopped there, but for Lewis it was only the beginning.

He won gold medals in four Olympics (1984, 1988, 1992, and 1996), capturing 10 Olympic medals in all. Nine of them were gold, with the last medal coming at the age of 35 in Atlanta in 1996.

"He was the Babe Ruth and Michael Jordan of our sport," Pete Cava of the United States Track Federation told writer Michael Point.

"You always tried harder when Carl was competing," said American sprinter Leroy Burrell. "Part of it was the natural urge to win, but a lot of it was because you didn't want to get embarrassed."

Tom Tellez, Lewis' coach at the University of Houston, put it very simply: "He's the greatest athlete I've ever seen."

---

the first Major League Baseball strike in history began. Players walked out over a pension dispute. The strike was settled on April 13, and the season began on April 15, 10 days late.

As more players became free agents (that is, they had the right to negotiate with any team when their contract expired), salaries soared sky high. At the same time, television revenues grew increasingly more important in the financial structure of the game. Labor disputes between players and owners became what seemed like an annual event.

The 1981 strike was different. It was baseball's first midseason strike. Never

Ali's Last Fight

In the end, Muhammad Ali sat slumped on the stool in his corner, overweight, out of shape, and beaten badly by a Jamaican fighter named Trevor Berbick. It was an ignominious end to boxing's most storied career.

Ali had gone to the Bahamas to fight Berbick on December 11 because, with the three-time heavyweight champion's health declining, no place in the United States would sanction another fight. Berbick, who lost a title fight to Larry Holmes in April of 1981, easily won a unanimous 10-round decision.

The loss was only the fifth in 61 career fights for Ali, but it was his third defeat in his last four fights. He knew his career was at the end. The next day, he retired. "Father Time has caught up with me," he said. "I'm finished."

That was only partially true. While he was undoubtedly finished in the ring, Ali remained in the public eye as a goodwill ambassador the world over. A popular, but controversial figure, during his career, his popularity continued to grow in his post-boxing days without the accompanying controversy.

He remained an active public figure despite being diagnosed with Parkinson's Syndrome, brought on by the years of hits he took while boxing.

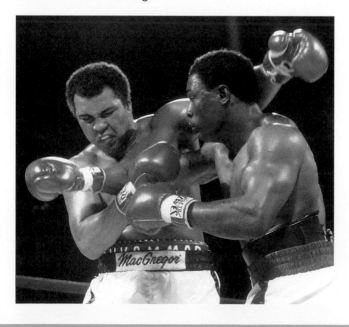

before had the game been wrenched away from fans just as the pennant races were heating up. By the time it ended, the 1981 work stoppage was the longest strike in American sports history, shutting down the game for 50 days and wiping out more than a third of the season.

The main issue of the dispute was compensation for free agents. Today's baseball fan is used to seeing players leave their team when a contract is up to sign with a new team as a free agent—and the team they left receives nothing in return. But in 1981, the idea and practice of free agency was still very new. Owners felt that when a player left their team, some type of compensation was in order.

The players had fought for and won, at the bargaining table and in the courts, the right to become free agents without any compensation going back to the team they left. But the owners wanted to take back the players' victory, feeling they deserved something in return for players they lost to free agency.

To the players, this was totally unacceptable. After fighting for years to obtain free-agent status, they were not about to give up that hard-fought victory. And so the strike dragged on. Although they had called the strike, the players grew bitter, blaming the owners for the lost baseball games. Older players grew frustrated as they tried to add to their career statistics. Younger players wanted to play a full season so they could continue developing their skills and establishing themselves.

And fans lost, perhaps most of all. For a baseball fan, the games are an inseparable part of the summer. Not being able to go to ballpark, or catch a game on

Other Milestones of 1981

✔ Mike Bossy of the New York Islanders became only the second player in NHL history to score 50 goals in the first 50 games of the season, tying Maurice ("the Rocket") Richard, who pulled off the feat in the 1944–45 season.

✔ On April 12, boxing great Joe Louis (1914–1981) died at age 66. Louis, who was known as the Brown Bomber, reigned as the heavyweight champion from 1937 to 1949.

✔ Jockey Bill Shoemaker won his record 8,000th race on May 27, far more than any other jockey in history.

✔ The longest game in baseball history was finally completed two months after it began. On April 18 the Pawtucket Red Sox and the Rochester Red Wings of the International League (a minor league) played 32 innings before the game was finally stopped at 4:07 the next morning. The game was completed on June 23, when Pawtucket scored in the 33rd inning for a 3–2 victory.

Nolan Ryan

✔ In a September 26 game against the Los Angeles Dodgers, Houston Astros pitcher Nolan Ryan (b.1947) threw his record breaking fifth no-hitter, surpassing Sandy Koufax's mark of four. Ryan eventually finished his baseball career with an astounding seven no-hitters.

✔ Pat Riley (b.1945) took over as coach of basketball's Los Angeles Lakers and led them to four more NBA titles in the 1980s. He took the team to the NBA Finals seven of the next eight seasons.

---

television or radio, caused bitterness and anger toward both players and owners.

With the season approaching the point of cancellation, Marvin Miller, head of the Players' Association (the players' labor union), finally worked out a complex agreement that extended baseball's Basic Agreement, signed in 1980 between players and owners, without actually resolving the free-agent compensation issue.

All told, the strike caused the cancellation of 706 games (38 percent of the season), and cost the players $28 million and the owners $116 million. The owners, however, had taken out strike insurance, which made up for some of that loss.

The decision was made to turn 1981 into a split season. The teams that were in first place in their respective divisions on June 11, when the last games were played, were declared winners of the first half of the season. A new "second season" began on August 10. All teams started with a 0–0 record. The teams that finished in first place over the second half of the season would meet the teams that won their divisions in the first half, in a best-of-five playoff series.

The unusual split season set 1981 apart from all other baseball seasons. No team was hurt more by the split season than the Cincinnati Reds, who finished with the best overall record in baseball but didn't make the playoffs. They finished a close second in each half of the split season.

1982

Playoff Marathon

After the San Diego Chargers had finally outlasted the Miami Dolphins 41–38 in overtime of their AFC Divisional Playoff Game on January 2, tight end Kellen Winslow's San Diego teammates had to help him to the locker room (see page 25). It has become one of the most iconic images in NFL history—a fitting snapshot of one of the most dramatic, exciting and memorable games ever.

Winslow, a future member of the Pro Football Hall of Fame, literally was exhausted after helping his team pull out the victory. He caught 13 passes for 166 yards and a touchdown, and blocked a field-goal try in the final seconds of the fourth quarter that could have won it for the Dolphins. "Thank God it's over," he told his teammates. "It's the closest to death I've ever been."

Indeed, the game ended up pushing the physical, mental and emotional limits of the players, coaches, and even the fans.

San Diego jumped out to a 24–0 lead in the first quarter and appeared to be unstoppable. The Chargers racked up the points on a 32-yard field goal by Rolf Benirschke, a 56-yard punt return by Wes Chandler, a one-yard touchdown run by Chuck Muncie, and an eight-yard touchdown pass from quarterback Dan Fouts to running back James Brooks.

In the second quarter, Miami coach Don Shula replaced starting quarterback David Woodley with Don Strock. Strock brought Miami back into the game, engineering a long drive that resulted in a field goal, then tossing three touchdown passes to tie the game in the third period.

Fouts came right back with a 25-yard touchdown pass to Winslow, but Miami tied the score again when Strock connected with Bruce Hardy on a 50-yard touchdown pass. Early in the fourth quarter, Miami took its first lead of the game on a 12-yard touchdown run by Tony Nathan. Then, with 58 seconds left in the fourth quarter, Fouts forced an overtime period by finding James Brooks with a nine-yard touchdown pass to tie the game at 38–38. As time expired, Miami's Uwe von Schamann attempted a potential game-winning field goal, but Winslow blocked it.

In overtime, where the first score meant victory, Schamann had another field-goal attempt blocked by the Chargers. San Diego's kicker, Rolf Benirschke,

Working Overtime *San Diego Chargers tight end Kellen Winslow (80) is helped off the field by his teammates after a marathon NFL playoff victory over the Miami Dolphins.*

missed a field goal in the overtime period, as well. Finally, after 13 minutes, 29 seconds of overtime play, Benirschke kicked a 29-yard field goal to give San Diego the victory.

Both quarterbacks were amazing in a game that, unfortunately, someone had to lose. Fouts threw for 433 yards and three touchdowns, while Strock racked up 403 yards and four touchdowns.

1982

Montana Looks Super

The San Francisco 49ers, the worst team in the NFL in the late 1970s, completed an amazingly quick turn-around by winning the league championship for the first time in the 1981 season. They capped their resurgence with a 26–21 victory over the Cincinnati Bengals in Super Bowl XVI at the Silverdome in Pontiac, Michigan, on January 24.

San Francisco quarterback Joe Montana (b.1956) was named the game's most valuable player. Although Montana's statistics were not spectacular in this game— he passed for 157 yards and a touchdown and ran for another touchdown—he operated the 49ers' offense efficiently and flawlessly. In fact, there arguably has never been a quarterback who operated with as much calm and grace in the most pressure-filled situations as Montana. It's almost as if he preferred to have the game or the season on the line with under a minute to go, 80 yards away from the winning touchdown. At the very least, he thrived on those high-pressure situations. By the time the decade ended, his would be a familiar face peering over center, coolly barking out signals, doing whatever needed to be done to bring victory in the biggest games.

The 49ers went on to win a total of four Super Bowls in the 1980s under Montana's leadership, clearly establishing themselves as the team of the decade. In his and the team's first Super Bowl, they faced another first-time entry in the Bengals. Both San Francisco and Cincinnati won only six games in the 1980 season before winning division titles in 1981.

San Francisco was fresh off a dramatic 28–27 victory over the Dallas Cowboys in the NFC title game. To pull that one out, Montana had tossed a six-yard touchdown pass to a leaping Dwight Clark in the back of the end zone with 51 seconds left in the game. Cincinnati routed San Diego 27–7 for the AFC title.

Although both teams were in the big game for the first time, Cincinnati really looked like the rookie squad, committing three turnovers in the first half, which the 49ers converted into 17 points en route to a 20–0 halftime edge. The first two turnovers—a Dwight Hicks interception and a Lynn Thomas fumble recovery—occurred deep in the 49ers' own territory. Both led to long scoring drives.

In the second half, Cincinnati quarterback Ken Anderson brought the Bengals back to within six points, but a couple of San Francisco field goals sealed the 49ers' first Super Bowl victory. They took the game by a score of 26–21.

The championship marked a tremendous turnaround for Montana and the 49ers, led by coach Bill Walsh.

Walsh inherited a team that had been 2–14 in 1978 when he took over in 1979. The 49ers went 2–14 again that year but were much improved offensively. Then, the season before their Super Bowl victory, the team finished with a 6–10 record. But in 1981, Walsh made Montana, a third-round draft pick in 1981, his full-time starting quarterback. Montana passed for 3,565 yards and 19 touchdowns, and the 49ers finished the regular season with a 13–3 record—the best in the league—which they followed up with their victory in the Silverdome.

The Shot

Although their future NBA battles would dominate the league in the 1990s, when Michael Jordan (b.1963) and Patrick Ewing (b.1962) faced off in the NCAA championship game on March 29, they were both just college freshman.

Ewing's Georgetown University team counted on the seven-foot-tall center's tough inside defense, rebounding and scoring. Jordan's University of North Carolina teammates looked to him to consistently hit his jump shots, racking up points.

Georgetown had a 32–31 lead at halftime. The second half featured fiercely competitive play, and neither team built up more than a four-point lead. Eric Smith and Sleepy Floyd added offense to Ewing's effort for Georgetown, while Jordan's jumpers and James Worthy's hard drives and defense kept North Carolina in the game.

Floyd gave Georgetown its last lead of the game when he hit a jump shot to put his team up 62–61 with 57 seconds left. North Carolina ran 25 seconds off the clock, then called a timeout to set up one final play.

Everyone in the building expected the play to go to Worthy, a junior and the team's leader. But North Carolina coach Dean Smith surprised Georgetown and showed great confidence in his freshman player by designing a play for Jordan.

With 15 seconds on the clock, Jordan did what he would come to do so many times during the years in which he dominated the NBA. He calmly hit a 16-foot jump shot, which proved to be the game winner.

Air Apparent *Before he became an international superstar, Michael Jordan led North Carolina to an NCAA championship.*

Looking for the ball with the game on the line and coming through in the clutch became Jordan's trademarks while helping the Chicago Bulls dominate the NBA in the 1990s. But he set the pattern way back in his freshman year at North Carolina, in the first of his many championship games.

1982

The Great One

Some athletes redefine what people thought was possible in a sport. In hockey, Wayne Gretzky rewrote the record books in the 1980s.

Gretzky scored an unheard-of 212 total points (goals plus assists) in the 1981–82 season, breaking his own NHL single-season record by 51 points.

In addition to his record for total points, Gretzky set a slew of other NHL single-season records: most goals (92), most assists (120), most hat tricks (three goals in a single game—he had 10), and highest points-per-game average (2.65).

On his way to 212 points, Gretzky passed Phil Esposito's 76 goals in one season record, as well as his own assists record of 109. He scored five goals in one game, and four goals in a game three times. In an 82-game season, Gretzky was held scoreless only eight times. His team, the Edmonton Oilers, had the second best record in the NHL.

Gretzky, at the age of 21, won the MVP award, his third in three years.

Women's Hoops

In March 1982, the NCAA held its first women's championship basketball tournament. This was not, however, the first basketball championship for women. In 1972, the Association for Intercollegiate Athletics for Women

Born to Skate

Wayne Gretzky learned to skate at the age of two. Growing up in Brantford, Ontario, in Canada, young Gretzky learned the fundamentals of hockey from his father, Walter. By the age of six, he was already considered a prodigy, playing against 10-year-olds. At the age of eight, he scored 104 goals in a season, playing against 13-year-olds. At age 10 he scored 378 goals in 82 games.

When Gretzky reached the age of 15, he was already playing top level junior league hockey, always the youngest, yet always the best on his teams. He signed his first professional contract at age 17, playing for the World Hockey Association's Indianapolis Racers, who traded him to the WHA's Edmonton Oilers.

In 1979, the Oilers were accepted into the NHL and Gretzky began changing what was possible to achieve in hockey, setting new records each passing season.

Oilers coach Billy Harris said of Gretzky's 212-point 1981–82 season, "That's like rushing for 3,000 yards or hitting 80 home runs in a season."

It wasn't his overpowering physique that intimidated opponents. Gretzky was not particularly strong, nor fast, nor did he have a devastating slap shot. What he had was uncanny instinct for seeing what was going to happen before it happened, for knowing where a teammate would be and getting a pass there, and for avoiding hard hits from the defense.

"Gretzky sees a picture out there that no one else sees," Boston Bruins executive Harry Sinden told ESPN. "It's difficult to describe, because I've never seen the game he's looking at."

(AIAW) held the first national women's college basketball tournament. At that time, the NCAA was not involved in women's sports. But by 1981, the NCAA began to stage a number of championships for women in tournaments that competed with the AIAW.

This year's tournament started with a 32-team field. Eventually, Louisiana Tech University beat Cheyney University of Pennsylvania by a score of 76–62 for the title. That first NCAA championship game drew 9,351 fans. The entire tournament brought in 56,320 people. Within a few years, that number had doubled, as women's college sports began to come into their own in the 1980s.

Before the NCAA got involved with women's college basketball, most of the best teams came from small, unknown colleges, like the two that made it to the finals that year. With the NCAA's involvement, many larger schools began taking their women's athletic programs more seriously.

We're Number One! *Forward Ann Pendergrass and her Louisiana Tech teammates won the first NCAA women's basketball championship by beating Cheyney University in the final game.*

Watson's Day at the Beach

Tom Watson beat Jack Nicklaus in a dramatic duel in the final round of golf's U.S. Open in June at Pebble Beach, California. Watson won with one of the most memorable shots in golf history.

After 16 holes of the last round, Watson and Nicklaus were tied atop the leaderboard. Then, on the par-three 17th, Watson's tee shot landed beyond the green in heavy, treacherous rough. He was only about 15 feet from the hole, but a delicate pitch shot could have cost him the tournament if not executed properly—too

short, and he's still in the rough; too long, and he could bogey the hole. "Get it close," Watson's caddy told him. "No, I'm going to make it," Watson replied.

And he did. As Watson's pitch trickled into the cup, he danced around the green in joy. Watson went on to birdie the 18th hole also to win by two shots.

The next month, Watson completed a rare feat when he followed his U.S. Open triumph by winning the British Open.

1982

The Specter of Drugs

More and more as the decades of the 20th century unfolded, sports came to reflect what was happening in the rest of American society. As drug use increased, the dark specter of substance abuse raised its terrifying head in the world of sports.

How much was known of cocaine use in the NFL in the 1980s is hard to say. Did players hide it from each other? From coaches? From team officials? Or was there an unspoken "look the other way" policy?

When the July 14 issue of *Sports Illustrated* magazine hit the newsstands in 1982, a bright light was shed on this dark secret. Don Reese, a retired defensive end who had played for the Miami Dolphins (1974–76), the New Orleans Saints (1978–80) and the San Diego Chargers (1981), told the magazine that cocaine "now controls and corrupts" NFL football, because so many players in the league used it.

Reese himself was sentenced in 1977 to one year in prison for selling cocaine. He called the problem a growing cancer in the league. "Cocaine can be found in quantity throughout the NFL," Reese said in the article, which he co-wrote with *Sports Illustrated* staff writer John Underwood. "It's pushed on players, often from the edge of the practice field. Sometimes it's pushed by players. Prominent players. A cocaine cloud covers the entire league. I think most coaches know this or have a good idea."

Reese told of his own drug use, which included free-basing (inhaling cocaine in a smokable form) with several other members of the Saints. At the time of the article, Reese still owed $30,000 to drug dealers and said he had been threatened by these dealers several times.

In 1980, the NFL had introduced a voluntary program to enable players with drug and alcohol problems to find help. As of 1982, 17 players had taken advantage of the program. As cocaine use spiraled out of control in America during the 1980s, its effect on sports grew as well, and could no longer be ignored.

Decker: Another Record

Mary Decker already owned the world record for the fastest time in the women's 5,000-meter race, the 3,000-meter race, the 2,000-meter race, and the 800-meter race when she took off in the 10,000-meters at Hayward Field in her hometown of Eugene, Oregon, on July 16.

One week earlier at an international meet in Paris, Decker set a new women's world record in the mile, turning in a time of four minutes, 18.08 seconds. Now, with the hometown crowd cheering her on, she set a world record in the 10,000, finishing in 31 minutes, 35.30 seconds. The 10,000-meter race had been dominated by Soviet women, who held the nine fastest times in the event, before Decker's world-record run.

As "Little Mary Decker" (she was only 4-foot-10, 86 pounds), she burst onto the international track and field scene in 1973 at a United States-Soviet meet in Minsk. Her breakthrough year was 1980, when she set three world records. Later, she went on to win the 1,500- and 3,000-meter races at the 1983 World Championships in Helsinki, Finland.

But 1982 was the finest year of her career, when she set records in the 2,000-, 3,000-, 5,000-, and 10,000-meter races, as well as her triumph in the mile. For her achievements, Decker was voted the Women's Sports Foundation's Amateur Sportswoman of the Year. She also won the Jesse Owens Award, which is presented annually to the best U.S. track and field athlete. She became the first woman to win that prestigious award.

Magical Mark

A total of 300 victories is the magical number for Major League Baseball starting pitchers, only 23 of whom reached that plateau through 2009. No relief pitchers ever reached 300 career saves, however, until the Milwaukee Brewers' Rollie Fingers reached that mark on August 21. That night, Fingers pitched the final two innings of the Brewers' 3–2 victory over the Mariners at the Kingdome in Seattle.

Fingers was in his 15th big-league season then and was just five days short of his 36th birthday. The American League Cy Young Award winner and Most Valuable Player the previous season for Milwaukee, Fingers first came to prominence as an All-Star for the powerful Oakland A's teams of the 1970s. He also pitched four seasons for the San Diego Padres, and in 1985 finished his career in Milwaukee with a record 341 saves.

As relief pitchers have taken on a greater role in today's game and closers are used almost exclusively in the ninth inning, 300 saves no longer is such an unattainable milestone. Some 21 relief pitchers in all have reached the mark entering 2010, although Fingers' total since ranks No. 10 all-time.

King of Steals

The Oakland Athletics' Rickey Henderson (b.1958)—baseball's all-time stolen base leader and the man considered by many to be the greatest leadoff hitter the game has ever seen—broke the single-season stolen base record on August 27 in a game at Milwaukee against the Brewers.

Henderson broke the record that had been set by St. Louis Cardinals' great Lou Brock, who stole 118 bases in 1974. Henderson stole base number 119 in the third inning, after drawing a walk from Brewers pitcher Doc Medich. Medich tossed over to first four times to chase Henderson

Top Base-Stealing Seasons of the 20th Century

PLAYER	TEAM	SEASON	STOLEN BASES
Rickey Henderson	Oakland Athletics	1982	130
Lou Brock	St. Louis Cardinals	1974	118
Vince Coleman	St. Louis Cardinals	1985	110
Vince Coleman	St. Louis Cardinals	1987	109
Rickey Henderson	Oakland Athletics	1983	108
Vince Coleman	St. Louis Cardinals	1986	107
Maury Wills	Los Angeles Dodgers	1962	104
Rickey Henderson	Oakland Athletics	1980	100
Ron Leflore	Montreal Expos	1980	97
Ty Cobb	Detroit Tigers	1915	96

Other Milestones of 1982

✔ Carl Lewis broke the 28-foot mark in the long jump in January, setting a new world record. He leapt a distance of 28 feet, 1 inch, in the United States Olympic Invitational track meet.

✔ On January 26, Cheryl Miller, future NCAA basketball great, scored 105 points in a high school game for Riverside Polytechnic in California. Miller went on to play college basketball at the University of Southern California, where she led the Women of Troy to a pair of national championships in the 1980s.

✔ Martina Navratilova (b.1956) began her incredible run in women's tennis by winning 90 of 93 matches.

✔ Sugar Ray Leonard retired from boxing due to an eye injury. His record was 32–1, with 22 knockouts. His only loss came at the hands of Roberto Duran (see page 16).

✔ Lorri Bauman of the Drake University Bulldogs scored 50 points in a West Regional basketball game against the University of Maryland. Although Maryland won that game 89–78 to advance to the Final Four, Bauman's total still stands as the most points ever scored in an NCAA women's tournament game.

✔ Steve Carlton of the Philadelphia Phillies, who won 23 games at age 37, became the first pitcher to win four Cy Young Awards.

✔ Shirley Muldowney won her third National Hot Rod Association points title—the only driver, male or female, to ever win three.

Shirley Muldowney

✔ Kathy Whitworth was inducted into the World Golf Hall of Fame. Her 88 career victories are the most by an American.

✔ The Supreme Court ruled that Title IX covers coaches and other school employees as well as students. Title IX is a federal regulation that mandates equal funding for boys' and girls' programs, including athletic programs, at schools in the United States.

✔ Tear-away jerseys appeared for the first time in college football. A tear-away jersey easily tears off when grabbed by an opposing player, so that the wearer can't be pulled down by his jersey.

back to the bag. He then threw a pitchout to catcher Ted Simmons as Henderson started for second. The throw by Simmons to Brewers shortstop Robin Yount was a good one, but Henderson slid in under the tag and was safe at second.

The game was stopped and members of both teams and the media gathered around Henderson at second base. The Oakland speedster pulled the base from the ground and held it over his head triumphantly. Henderson went on to steal three more bases in that game, and finished the season with 130, still the modern single-season record. He eventually played through the 2003 season, and ended his 25-year career with 1,406 thefts, another record.

NFL Strike Is the Longest

For the first time in NFL history, players staged a strike that interrupted the regular-season schedule. The strike began on September 21, two games into the 1982 season. By the time it ended 57 days later, on November 16, it had become the longest strike in professional sports history, surpassing the baseball strike of 1981 by seven days. (The baseball strike of 1994, which led to the cancellation of the playoffs and World Series, is the current record holder. It lasted 234 days.)

As with the 1981 baseball strike, the issue was money. And once again, as would happen more and more frequently in the 1980s and beyond, fans turning to the sports page would come to read about labor negotiations, team revenues, and player salaries, instead of games won and lost. Sports was business, and the business of sports had grown so big by the 1980s that at times the games seemed secondary to financial deals and labor disputes.

One major issue in this strike was the fact that before 1982 the NFL Players Association (the players' labor union) was not allowed to receive copies of players' contracts. After the strike, contracts and salaries were a more open issue, as the union was allowed to receive all contract information. Minimum salaries were established, and free-agency was expanded.

When the strike was finally settled, the decision was made to reduce the number of games in the 1982 season to nine—the two played before the strike, plus seven more after. In addition, 16 teams qualified for the playoffs (six more than usual), and the regular season ended a week later than originally scheduled.

The strike cost the league $240 million in lost ticket and television money, and wiped 112 games from the schedule. The resulting agreement was set to last until 1986 and brought the players $60 million in bonuses, plus $1.3 billion in salaries and benefits for the years 1983–86.

Attendance for the games played after the strike was down greatly, and it took almost a full year for fans to return to the NFL in pre-strike numbers.

Bye-Bye Oakland

Controversial Oakland Raiders owner Al Davis wanted to move his team from Oakland to Los Angeles. The NFL said no. As was becoming the case more and more often in sports in the 1980s, the two sides ended up in court.

Davis sued, claiming an antitrust violation, saying the league had no right to tell him where he could or couldn't move his team. Following a long and bitter court battle, a jury awarded Davis the right to move his team to Los Angeles.

And so, before the 1982 season, Davis moved his Raiders about 500 miles south. The team began playing its home games in the Los Angeles Coliseum instead of the Oakland Coliseum. (The franchise eventually reversed course in 1995 and went back up north to Oakland.)

The ruling shook up the NFL, which saw moves by the Cleveland Browns, Los Angeles Rams, and Houston Oilers in the years that followed this decision.

1983

Riggins' Run

The Washington Redskins' John Riggins capped a remarkable postseason performance with one of the most memorable runs in Super Bowl history on January 30. Riggins raced 43 yards for the go-ahead touchdown in the fourth quarter of his team's 27–17 victory over the Miami Dolphins in Super Bowl XVII at Pasadena, California.

Riggins, the Redskins' burly fullback, carried his team through the longest postseason in NFL history. Because of the strike-shortened regular season (see page 33), the postseason was expanded to include 16 teams in a single-elimination tournament. Riggins rushed for 610 yards and four touchdowns in Washington's four postseason wins, including 166 yards and the key fourth-quarter score against the Dolphins.

Washington trailed Miami 17–13 until Riggins' decisive run came on a fourth-down-and-one play with 10:01 remaining in the game. The Redskins added an insurance touchdown late in the fourth quarter.

Riggins was named the game's most valuable player.

Big Name to New League

The United States Football League (USFL) began play in 1983. Playing a 16-game schedule in the spring, so as not to go head-to-head with the NFL's fall season, the new league featured colorful owners and competed with the NFL for top college players.

Founded by David Dixon, a New Orleans art and antiques dealer, the USFL announced its formation on May 11, 1982. The USFL started with 12 teams in major markets across the country: New Jersey, Los Angeles, Chicago, Detroit, Boston, Tampa, Oakland, Denver, Washington, Philadelphia, Birmingham, and San Diego (that franchise moved to Phoenix). The games were shown on ESPN and ABC.

Shortly before the start of their inaugural season, the New Jersey Generals signed University of Georgia tailback Herschel Walker, 1982's Heisman Trophy winner (the Heisman Trophy is awarded annually to the best college football player in the nation). Walker left college a year early to turn pro, and the highly touted rookie gave credibility to the new league. During his college career, Walker rushed for 5,259 yards and set 10 NCAA records.

Super Run *Washington Redskins running back John Riggins sheds a would-be tackler and breaks free on the go-ahead touchdown run in the fourth quarter of Super Bowl XVII in Pasadena, California. The Redskins beat the Miami Dolphins 27–17.*

Walker's contract with New Jersey made him the highest paid player in football history. He received $1.5 million, compared to Chicago Bears running back Walter Payton (a future member of the Pro Football Hall of Fame), who had the top NFL salary of $700,000.

Although the USFL's level of play was not up to NFL quality, the teams averaged more than 24,000 fans a game. The ratings were also good. But huge player salaries put many teams into financial trouble—trouble that would plague the USFL throughout its entire existence.

Their Cup Runneth Over and Over and. . . *Winning the Stanley Cup championship was getting to be old hat for captain Dennis Potvin and the New York Islanders, who won their fourth straight NHL title.*

Islanders Win Again

Since the formation of the NHL in 1917, no team has dominated the league the way the Montreal Canadiens have. In hockey, the word "dynasty" usually means Montreal. The Canadiens have won the Stanley Cup championship 23 times since then (that's by far a league record; the next closest, the Toronto Maple Leafs, stand at just 13 championships). Between 1955 and 1960 the Canadiens won five consecutive Stanley Cups, a feat that has never been equaled. Then, from 1975 to 1979, the Canadiens won four straight Stanley Cups.

In 1983, the New York Islanders became just the second team in NHL history to win four Stanley Cups in a row, creating their own dynasty and joining Montreal in the record books.

The streak began with a Stanley Cup Championship in the 1979–80 season, when the Islanders beat the Philadelphia Flyers in six games in the finals. In 1980–81, the Isles (as their fans call them) beat the Minnesota North Stars in five games in the finals. The 1981–82 finals saw the Islanders sweep the Vancouver Canucks in four straight games.

New York took its fourth straight Cup in May, completing another four-game sweep in the 1982–83 finals by beating the Edmonton Oilers, who were led by the Great One, Wayne Gretzky. During the regular season, Gretzky scored 71 goals and had 196 points on the way to his fourth straight MVP award. But in the Stanley Cup finals, the Islanders tough defense shut down Gretzky and his Oilers' teammates.

The Oilers were held to just six goals in the four-game series, and they didn't score off Islanders goaltender Billy Smith in seven of the 12 periods played. Islanders Bryan Trottier and Butch Goring stuck close to Gretzky, limiting him to just four assists.

The Islanders' offense was led by Mike Bossy and Clark Gillies.

Watson Wins Fifth Open

American golfer Tom Watson won his fifth British Open golf championship in July. This achievement is unique in recent times, and places Watson second only to Harry Vardon, who won six British Opens between the years 1896 and 1914.

Watson took the Open with a combined four-round total of 275 at the Royal Birkdale course in England. His other victories in the British Open came in 1975, 1977, 1980, and 1982.

Watson joined the PGA Tour in 1971, and was the leading money winner on the Tour in 1977, 1978, 1979, 1980, and 1984. He was voted PGA Player of the Year six times (1977, 1978, 1979, 1980, 1982, and 1984), and was a member of four United States Ryder Cup teams (1977, 1981, 1983, and 1989). He served as captain in 1993.

Watson also won the Vardon Trophy (named for Harry Vardon) three years in a row (1977–79). The Vardon Trophy is awarded by the PGA of America to the PGA Tour regular with the lowest average score for the year.

Malone Leads 76ers

Center Moses Malone scored 24 points and grabbed 23 rebounds to lead the Philadelphia 76ers to a 115–108 victory over the Los Angeles Lakers on May 31 in Los Angeles. The 76ers' victory capped a four-game sweep in the NBA Finals and ended the Lakers' reign as the league champs.

It was fitting that Malone was the key player in the decisive game because he was the man that the 76ers tabbed in free agency to team with Julius Erving, the 76ers' perennial All-Star, for the 1982–83 season. In these days of high-priced free agents, it doesn't seem unusual for a pro team to go out and spend millions to land the player they need. But in the 1980s, the concept was still new.

The Philadelphia 76ers had not won an NBA title since 1967. Team owner Harold Katz decided to go out and buy a top star to team with Erving.

The 6-foot-10 Malone had been the first player to go straight from high school into pro basketball, without going to college. Like Erving, Malone began his pro career in the American Basketball Association (ABA), a rival league that eventually merged several of its teams into the NBA.

From 1974 to 1976, Malone was a dominant center, a powerful rebounder, and a prolific scorer for the ABA's Utah Stars and St. Louis Spirit. When the two leagues merged in 1976, Malone joined the Buffalo Braves, then later played for the Houston Rockets, where he continued to be among the league leaders in scoring and rebounding. Following the 1981–82 season, he became a free agent.

Determined to bring a championship home to the loyal fans in Philadelphia, Katz gave Malone a contract worth $13.2 million over four years, an unheard-of figure in the NBA at that time. But it paid off. During the regular season, Malone averaged 24.5 points and a league-leading 15.3 rebounds per game. Those numbers only improved during the playoffs, when Malone averaged 25.8 points and 18.5 rebounds per game while leading the 76ers to 12 wins in 13 postseason games.

1983

The Pine Tar Incident

It was surely one of baseball's strangest and most controversial moments. On July 24, the Kansas City Royals were at Yankee Stadium, playing just another regular-season game against the Bronx Bombers. With two outs and nobody on base in the top of the ninth inning, the Yankees led 4–3. The Royals' U.L. Washington hit a single, bringing up Kansas City third baseman George Brett.

Brett smashed a two-run homer off Yankees relief pitcher Goose Gossage, giving the Royals a 5–4 lead. Or so everyone in the stadium thought.

Once Brett crossed home plate and had gone into the Kansas City dugout, however, Yankees manager Billy Martin walked up to home plate umpire Tim McClelland and handed him Brett's bat, complaining that the bat was illegal because it had too much pine tar. Pine tar is a dark, sticky substance that players put onto their bat handles to get a better grip. While use of the pine tar is legal, the amount a player may use is specified in the rules. A player may not place any substance on his bat to improve the grip that extends more than 18 inches from the end of the bat handle.

The umpires all met around home plate, measuring the amount of pine tar on the bat against the front side of home plate (which they knew to be 17 inches long). The umpires ruled that there was more than 18 inches of pine tar on the bat, and so McClelland signaled that Brett was out and the home run did not count.

The Royals' third baseman sprang from the dugout, racing toward McClelland, his eyes bulging with rage, a stream of obscenities pouring from his lips. Umpiring crew chief Joe Brinkman intercepted Brett before he reached McClelland, grabbing him around the neck and trying to calm him down. Royals manager Dick Howser and coach Rocky Colavito joined the fray and were soon ejected from the game along with Brett.

Meanwhile, Brett's Kansas City teammate, future Hall-of-Fame pitcher Gaylord Perry, slipped out of the dugout, grabbed the bat, and headed for the clubhouse to hide it. Perry was stopped by stadium security, who took the bat back and ejected Perry from the stadium.

The home run was nullified, and the Yankees won the game 4–3. Or so everyone at the stadium thought. But the Royals protested the decision, arguing that there was no intentional plan to cheat and that they did not violate the spirit of the rules. American League president Lee MacPhail agreed. He overruled the umpires' deci-

The Pine-Tar Rule

Rule 1.10 (c) of the official baseball rulebook states:

The bat handle, for not more than 18 inches from its end, may be covered or treated with any material or substance to improve the grip. Any such material or substance, which extends past the 18-inch limitation, shall cause the bat to be removed from the game.

Following the George Brett pine-tar incident, this rule was amended to read:

NOTE: If the umpire discovers that the bat does not conform to (c) above until a time during or after which the bat has been used in play, it shall not be grounds for declaring the batter out, or ejected from the game.

sion, stating that the game should resume from the point at which the pine-tar incident occurred—in other words, after Brett's home run, which would now count, and give the Royals a 5–4 lead.

Twenty-five days after it began, on August 18 (an open date for both teams), the "pine-tar game" resumed at Yankee Stadium in front of only 1,245 fans. Kansas City's Hal McRae made the final out in the top of the ninth inning, then Royals pitcher Dan Quisenberry set the Yankees down 1-2-3 in the bottom of the ninth inning to give Kansas City the victory.

Following this incident, baseball's rule book was amended to prevent a similar situation from occurring again (see the box on the opposite page).

When Brett was elected to the Baseball Hall of Fame in 1999, the famous pine tar bat went to Cooperstown with him, where it was placed on display.

Martina's First U.S. Open

Continuing her meteoric rise to the top of women's tennis, Martina Navratilova defeated Chris Evert-Lloyd on September 10 to capture her first U.S. Open singles championship. In a match that lasted only 63 minutes, Navratilova crushed Evert-Lloyd 6–1, 6–3. Cementing her stature as the top women's tennis player in the world, Navratilova dominated her opponent, top rival, and friend, rushing the net after nearly every serve, keeping Evert-Lloyd from setting up on the baseline.

The victory was Navratilova's 66th in her last 67 matches. By the end of 1983 she posted a record of 86–1, to follow the

On Top of the World *Martina Navratilova left no doubt that she was the best women's tennis player in the world with an easy, straight-sets victory over Chris Evert in the finals of the U.S. Open.*

90–3 record she put up in 1982. The former Czech defector (now an American) continued to dominate women's tennis throughout the 1980s with an aggressive and intimidating style that changed the face of the game (see box on page 40).

39

1983

Coaching Giants

The football world lost two of its coaching icons in 1983: On January 26, Alabama's Paul (Bear) Bryant (1913–1983) died at 69; on October 31, the Chicago Bears' George Halas (1895–1983) died at 88.

With 323 career victories, Bryant was the winningest coach in college football history at the time of his death. He had coached through the 1982 season, his 25th at Alabama and his 48th as a major-college coach in a career that began at Maryland in 1945. He also made stops at Kentucky (1946–1953) and Texas A & M (1954–57). It was at Alabama, though, that he really made his mark, wearing his trademark houndstooth hat while leading the Crimson Tide to six national championships and at least a share of 12 conference championships. Bryant died of heart failure only 28 days after he retired as Alabama's coach.

Halas was the founder and owner of the Bears, who were a charter member of the NFL (originally called the American Professional Football Association)

The Changing Face of Women's Tennis

Martina Navratilova's great contributions to the game of tennis can't be limited to her astounding 56 Grand Slam titles. (The Grand Slam is made up of tennis' four major tournaments: the Australian Open, the French Open, Wimbledon, and the U.S. Open.) She also took women's tennis to a new level of excitement and fan interest in the 1980s, bringing speed, power, and strength to the game. Navratilova introduced new training methods and nutritional programs specifically designed for female tennis players.

At age four, in her native Czechoslovakia, Navratilova got her first tennis racquet. At age six, she took her first lesson. When she was eight, she entered her first tournament. By the age of 16, she had become Czechoslovakia's top player.

In 1975, Navratilova defected to the United States, and by the mid-1980s she was well on her way to setting new standards for women's tennis. She changed the look and style of the women's game, making it faster and more athletic. After winning six Wimbledon titles in a row, from 1982 to 1987, to bring her total to eight, Navratilova returned to the finals in 1990 for her record-breaking ninth Wimbledon victory.

Her success inspired many girls, not only to become tennis players, but also to take part in athletics of many kinds. She had another impact off the court as well, beginning in 1981, when it became widely known, and she confirmed in interviews, that she was gay. Few athletes of her caliber have ever "come out of the closet," and she faced some criticism for her lifestyle. However, she battled against those opinions with the same power that she used to win on the court, and became an important spokesperson for the cause of fair treatment for gay and lesbian athletes.

Other Milestones of 1983

✔ San Diego Padres first baseman Steve Garvey played in his 1,118th consecutive baseball game on April 16, setting a new National League record. Garvey's streak eventually reached 1,207 games before ending in late July. It is the fourth-longest streak in big-league history.

✔ On May 31, Jack Dempsey (1895–1983), heavyweight boxing champ from 1919 to 1926, died at age 87.

✔ Rap music picked up sports culture as a theme when Grandmaster Flash released "The Message," in which he talked about "watching the game or the Sugar Ray fight." Also, rapper Kurtis Blow released the song "Basketball," a tribute to the NBA players he watched in the 1970s.

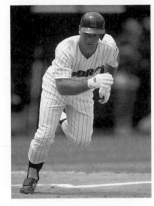

Steve Garvey

✔ Evelyn Ashford (b.1957) set a world record for women in the 100-meter run with a time of 10.79 seconds on July 3 at the National Sports Festival in Colorado Springs.

✔ Philadelphia Phillies pitcher Steve Carlton picked up his 300th career victory on September 23. Carlton struck out 12 batters in eight innings and beat the St. Louis Cardinals 6–2 to record his milestone win. Carlton went on to win 329 games in a 24-season career that ended in 1988. He was elected to the National Baseball Hall of Fame in 1994.

✔ Overtime for regular-season NHL games was reinstated for the first time since 1942, with a five-minute time limit. Before then, games simply ended in a tie.

---

in 1920 as the Decatur Staleys. The next year, Halas moved the team to Chicago, still with the name Staleys. In 1922, the club became known as the Bears. Halas coached the franchise for 40 years in four 10-year stints, winning six league championships and 324 games.

Three Royals Head to Jail

For the first time, three active Major League Baseball players were arrested and sent to jail on drug-related charges. On November 17, a federal judge sentenced Willie Wilson, Willie Aikens, and Jerry Martin of the Kansas City Royals to three-month jail sentences for attempting to purchase cocaine. All three had pleaded guilty.

Noting the special place in society he felt professional athletes held, the judge also fined Wilson and Aikens the maximum amount of $5,000, and he fined Martin $2,500. Martin and Aikens were released by the Royals. Wilson, the team's starting centerfielder, remained with the organization.

Commissioner Bowie Kuhn also suspended the players from baseball for one year, as the growing problem of illegal drug use among professional athletes leapt once again to the front page.

1984

Olympic Gold

On February 16, at the 1984 Winter Games in Sarajevo, Yugoslavia, Bill Johnson became the first American ever to win a gold medal in downhill skiing. That started an avalanche of skiing medals for the United States. Before the competition ended, the U.S. ski team took gold medals in three of the six downhill events—competition that had traditionally been dominated by European skiers. American brothers Phil and Steve Mahre followed Johnson's performance with gold and silver medal victories in the men's Alpine slalom. And not to be outdone, the American women's downhill team also pulled off a one-two finish.

The 23-year-old Johnson was born in Los Angeles, California, but he learned to ski in Idaho, where his family moved when he was a youngster. He was the U.S. champ in the downhill in 1983. At Sarajevo, Johnson tore down the 3,066-meter course in one minute, 45.59 seconds, beating Peter Mueller of Switzerland by 27-hundredths of a second. Johnson beat Mueller's time with a burst of speed just before he crossed the finish line.

Phil Mahre took the second U.S. downhill gold with a time of one minute, 39.41 seconds in the Alpine slalom, while Steve won the silver.

In the giant slalom, Debbie Armstrong captured the third U.S. downhill gold of the games with a time of two minutes, 20.98 seconds. American Christin Cooper took the silver.

The other notable performance by an American at the Sarajevo Games came from men's figure skater Scott Hamilton, who captured the gold in the men's individual competition. Hamilton became the first American to do so in 24 years.

The United States' ice hockey team was not as successful. The Americans were hoping to build on their "Miracle On Ice" victory at the 1980 Winter Olympics (see page 10), but the team failed to qualify for the medal round in Sarajevo.

Kareem Passes Wilt

There have been a handful of centers in the history of the NBA whose play was so dominant, whose sheer physical ability was so superior, that they changed the way the game is played. Teams had to adjust their strategies to stop these players from scoring, rebounding, or controlling the game on the defensive end of the court.

George Mikan of the Minneapolis Lakers was the first of this breed in the early days of the NBA. Bill Russell of the Boston Celtics helped his team build a championship dynasty in the 1950s and 1960s with his powerful shot blocking, rebounding and defense. Today, Shaquille O'Neal of the Cleveland Cavaliers fits the role of the dominant center who can single-handedly change the balance of any basketball game.

Among this elite group, two centers, both of whom began their pro careers elsewhere but eventually came to glory with the Lakers, rose above the rest offensively—Wilt Chamberlain in the 1960s and Kareem Abdul-Jabbar in the 1980s.

On April 5, Abdul-Jabbar hit his trademark skyhook—a high, arcing shot—with eight minutes, 53 seconds remaining in a game against the Utah Jazz. That brought his career scoring total to 31,421 points to surpass Chamberlain as the NBA's all-time leading scorer. (Chamberlain, who retired in 1973, scored 31,419 points during his 14-year NBA career.) The game was stopped and the crowd gave the 7-foot-2 center a long ovation.

While Chamberlain used his sheer size and awesome strength to dominate the league, Abdul-Jabbar used grace and a soft touch to beat his opponents. Following a spectacular college career, during which he led the University of California–Los Angeles (UCLA) to an 88–2 record and three national championships, Abdul-Jabbar joined the Milwaukee Bucks of the NBA and led them to the league championship

Sky Hook *Los Angeles Lakers center Kareem Abdul-Jabbar showcases his signature shot in a game against the Houston Rockets. Abdul-Jabbar became the NBA's all-time leading scorer in 1984.*

1984

in 1971. He joined the Lakers in 1975, and helped them win championships in 1980, 1982, 1985, 1987, and 1988.

Pat Riley, Abdul-Jabbar's coach with the Lakers, called his center's skyhook "the greatest weapon of one person who's ever been an athlete in any sport."

Seventh Heaven

The Boston Celtics won the NBA championship for the 15th time, beating the Los Angeles Lakers 111–102 in the seventh and deciding game of the Finals on June 12 in the Boston Garden.

The Celtics had never—and still haven't, entering 2010—lost a Game Seven in a championship series. They kept that streak going with a dominating performance on the boards against the Lakers. Boston's forwards, Cedric Maxwell and Larry Bird, and its center, Robert Parish, combined to pulled down 36 rebounds, more than the entire Lakers team.

In fact, Boston outrebounded Los Angeles by a commanding 52–33 margin.

Leading throughout, the Celtics scored the last six points of the game to lock up the victory. Maxwell scored 24 points, while Bird poured in 20. Kareem Abdul-Jabbar was the high scorer for the Lakers, with 29 points.

The Celtics and Lakers were familiar foes in the NBA playoffs—it was the eighth time they met in the Finals, and the eighth time the Celtics won—but it was their first meeting in the Magic Johnson–Larry Bird era.

The teams would meet again in the NBA Finals twice more in the next three seasons.

New NBA Commissioner

As the 1980s began, the popularity and reputation of the NBA was at a low. But the "Magic and Bird Show," re-igniting the classic Celtics-Lakers rivalry, coupled with the arrival of Chicago Bulls superstar Michael Jordan in 1985, jump-started interest in the league and began its revival.

Then David Stern took over as league commissioner. As it turned out, he was the perfect executive to maximize and capitalize on the league's growing popularity. First, he orchestrated a deal that created an NBA salary cap, setting a limit on how much each team could pay their players. This cap protected owners from endlessly skyrocketing payrolls, while guaranteeing players 53 percent of gross revenues. The agreement helped the NBA avoid the labor disputes that plagued baseball and football (and continue to plague baseball).

Under Stern's guidance, the league started marketing itself to a younger, more ethnically diverse fan base, tapping into hip-hop culture and consciously changing NBA basketball games into sports- and- entertainment events. The annual All-Star Game became All-Star Weekend, with popular slam-dunk and three-point contests, and the televised draft lottery increased fan interest in each year's crop of incoming college players.

With exciting, popular stars already in place, Stern was the final piece of the puzzle that brought the NBA to its greatest popularity in the 1980s and '90s. He entered his 26th season as league commissioner in 2009–10.

Payton Passes Brown

There had never been a football running back like Jim Brown (b.1936). He combined speed, balance, agility, and explosive power, making him almost impossible to tackle. "All you do," said former New York Giants linebacker Sam Huff when asked how he approached tackling Brown, "is grab hold, hang on, and wait for help."

During his nine seasons in the NFL (1957–1965) Brown led the league in rushing eight times, compiling a record 12,312 yards. After winning his second MVP award in 1965, Brown retired, preferring to go out at the top of his game.

On October 7, Brown's nearly 20-year-old career rushing record was shattered by the man they called "Sweetness." In the third quarter of a game against the New Orleans Saints, Chicago Bears

Sweetness

The Chicago Bears' Walter Payton combined amazing balance and power during his 13 years in the NFL (1975–1987) to rack up an astounding 16,726 rushing yards. That was a league record that stood until Dallas' Emmitt Smith surpassed it in 2002.

When a running back picks up 100 yards in a game, it's considered a great day. In a game against the Minnesota Vikings in 1977, Payton rushed for an NFL-record 275 yards. That mark stood for 23 years.

When faced with the choice between running out of bounds or colliding with a defensive player to try for a few extra yards, Payton put down his shoulder and bashed into his opponent, driving forward with an almost unstoppable force. He was as complete a player as has ever stepped onto a football field. In addition to his unmatched running ability, Payton also was a top-notch blocker and pass receiver. He could throw the ball well, too.

As intimidating as he was on the field, however, Payton earned his nickname "Sweetness" not only for his sweet moves, but also for his kind and playful temperament. Before Michael Jordan became

Walter Payton

Chicago's greatest sports hero, Payton was the most beloved athlete in town.

Sadly, in 1999, the Pro Football Hall of Famer (he was inducted in 1993, his first year of eligibility) was diagnosed with a rare liver disease. He died later that year shaking the entire sports world.

1984

running back Walter Payton took a pitchout (a play where the quarterback tosses the ball underhand to a back who is too far away to hand off to) from quarterback Jim McMahon and ran for six yards. Those yards pushed his 10-year career total past Brown's record.

When the game ended, Payton was mobbed by players from both teams, eager to offer congratulations to one of the most-loved professional athletes of all time (see the box on page 45). He finished that day with 154 yards, bringing his career total at the time to 12,400.

Payton broke another of Brown's records that day as well. He rushed for 100 yards or more for the 59th time of his career—one more than Brown had during his nine years in the NFL.

Colts Leave Town

The ever-tightening grip of business on sports was evident when, in a move that can only be described as sneaky, Baltimore Colts owner Robert Irsay moved his NFL franchise out of Baltimore and into Indianapolis on March 29, in the dead of night.

The secret operation stunned not only fans but also city officials, who, contrary to usual policy, had no idea the team planned to leave. Irsay, unhappy with his stadium lease and declining ticket sales in Baltimore, hired a fleet of vans to sneak over to the team's training facility and clean it out under cover of darkness. The vans then headed for Indianapolis, where Irsay decided to set up shop for the upcoming season. Indianapolis mayor William Hudnut announced the Colts' arrival,

saying the team would play their future NFL games in the yet-to-be-completed, 60,000-seat Hoosier Dome.

It was known that Irsay had been negotiating with city officials in Indianapolis for several months before the move, but the suddenness of the departure caught everyone by surprise. With the entire team's possessions already moved to Indianapolis, there was nothing the state of Maryland could do.

Having lost a court case that allowed the Oakland Raiders to move to Los Angeles in 1982 (see page 33), the NFL decided to keep a low profile and chose to take no action. Fans in Baltimore were stunned and outraged, and would remain so until the arrival of the NFL's Ravens in 1996.

Olympic Boycott

In an obvious payback for the U.S.-led boycott of the 1980 Olympics in Moscow, the Soviet Union and 13 of its allies boycotted the 1984 Summer Olympics in Los Angeles in August. Romania was the only Eastern European country in the Soviet bloc to come to Los Angeles. The powerhouse team from East Germany, always among the tops in medals, was among those that stayed away.

A record 140 nations did show up, but without the usual competition from the Soviets and East Germans, the United States won a record 83 gold medals.

The Los Angeles Olympics were the first privately financed games ever, and they made a huge profit of $215 million. *Time* magazine was so impressed that it named organizing president Peter Ueberroth its Man of the Year.

Good as Gold *Sixteen-year-old gymnast Mary Lou Retton (above) and sprinter Carl Lewis starred for the United States at the 1984 Olympic Games in Los Angeles.*

U.S. Men Take Gold

The American men's gymnastic team gave an inspired performance at the Summer Games in Los Angeles, capturing the gold medal in the all-around team competition.

The six-man squad of Peter Vidmar, Bart Conner, Mitch Gaylord, Tim Daggett, James Hartung, and Scott Johnson edged the world-champion Chinese team, which many thought was unbeatable, by just 0.6 points.

After five of the six events, the Americans held a small lead over the Chinese team. They were trying to win the first gold medal in gymnastics ever by a U.S. squad. Going with riskier but higher-scoring moves, the United States six held

together, finishing the final event, the horizontal bars, with a perfect 10 for Daggett. The gold was finally theirs!

Meanwhile, on the women's team, a 4-foot-9, 94-pound, 16-year-old named Mary Lou Retton led the American women to a silver medal in the team competition. She charmed the fans and instantly became America's sweetheart. Retton then took America's second gymnastics gold medal, becoming the first American woman to do so, by winning the individual all-around competition.

Retton wrapped up her performance with back-to-back perfect scores of 10 on both her vaults. Her inspired performance earned her Woman Athlete of the Year honors from the Associated Press for 1984.

1984

Lewis Wins Four Golds

U.S. track and field star Carl Lewis won gold medals at the Summer Olympics in Los Angeles in the same four events that Jesse Owens had won 48 years earlier at the 1936 Olympics in Berlin.

In the 100-meter sprint, Lewis came from behind to take the event in 9.99 seconds, beating his teammate, Sam Graddy. Next up was the long jump, where he leaped 28 feet, 1/4 inch on his first try. He passed on the remaining four jumps to conserve energy, and his jump held up for another gold. In the 200-meter sprint, Lewis led a United States sweep, winning the gold in 19.80 seconds—an Olympic record. American Kirk Baptiste took the silver with a time of 19.96 seconds, and Thomas Jefferson captured bronze with a time of 20.26 seconds to complete the U.S. sweep.

Lewis completed his grand slam as part of the 4-by-100-meter relay team, joining Graddy, Ron Brown, and Calvin Smith in setting a world record with a time of 37.83 seconds.

Women's Marathon

The first women's marathon in Olympic history was held at the Los

Other Milestones of 1984

✔ On April 13, Pete Rose became only the second player in baseball history to reach 4,000 career hits. He trailed only all-time hits leader Ty Cobb (1886–1961), who had 4,191 hits in his Major League Baseball career. Rose would pass Cobb in 1985 (see page 54).

✔ Kirk Gibson's World Series home run heroics helped the Detroit Tigers win the Series in five games. In game five on October 14, against the San Diego Padres, Gibson hit two homers and drove in five runs to lead the Tigers to an 8–4 Series-clinching victory.

✔ Martina Navratilova continued her dominance of women's tennis, winning 78 of her 80 matches.

Kirk Gibson

✔ The United States Supreme Court ruled that the NFL could not prevent its teams from moving from one city to another.

✔ The United States Supreme Court ruled that the NCAA's exclusive control over television coverage of college football violated the Sherman Antitrust Act, which outlaws monopolies.

✔ Miami Dolphins quarterback Dan Marino set NFL passing records with 5,084 yards and 48 touchdowns.

✔ Brigham Young won college football's national title, capping a 12–0 season with a 24–17 win over Michigan in Holiday Bowl on December 21.

Angeles Games on August 5. American Joan Benoit Samuelson, a two-time Boston Marathon winner and world-record holder in the event, won the inaugural race in two hours, 24 minutes, 53 seconds. Samuelson's gold medal time was not only the third best time ever run by a woman in any marathon, but would actually have taken the gold medal in 13 of the previous 20 Olympic marathons run by men.

Amazingly, America's newest golden hero almost didn't make it to the Games. Two and half weeks before the Olympic trials in May, she injured her right knee and underwent arthroscopic surgery. Intense physical therapy and cardiovascular conditioning (she pedaled an exercise bike with her hands) enabled her to win the Olympic trials just 17 days after her knee surgery.

As the first women's marathon in Olympic history began, many spectators lining the route wept with joy, realizing that the long struggle to achieve recognition for women's long-distance running had finally borne fruit. Just 14 minutes into the race, Samuelson pulled away from the pack and never looked back.

Half a mile from the Los Angeles Coliseum, where the long race would finally end, she passed a large mural depicting her victory at the Boston Marathon. As she entered the tunnel leading to the Coliseum's track, where she would complete her final lap, Benoit Samuelson hoped her achievement would announce to the world that women belonged among the ranks of great long-distance runners.

As she appeared in the stadium and took her final lap around the track, 50,000 screaming fans rose and cheered the lone figure who finished the race 400 meters (and more than minute) ahead of the rest of the field. The world of long-distance running would never be the same.

Women's Firms

Ten years after Little League Baseball officially opened its game to girls as well as boys, the first girl played in the Little League World Series. She was Victoria Roche, a backup outfielder for the team from Brussels, Belgium, that made it to Williamsport, Pennsylvania.

Women made their mark in the Naismith Memorial Basketball Hall of Fame in 1984, too. Senda Berenson Abbott, Bertha Teague, and Margaret Wade were the first women elected to the shrine.

Abbott was a native of Lithuania who immigrated to the United States. In 1899, she modified men's basketball rules for women, and in 1901 she wrote the first *Basketball Guide for Women*.

Teague was a legendary coach who was known as "Mrs. Basketball of Oklahoma." As coach at Byng High School in Ada, Oklahoma, from 1927 to 1969, she guided her teams to eight state championships, seven runner-up finishes, and an amazing winning percentage of .910 (1,157 wins and only 115 losses).

Wade was a star player and coach at both her prep (Cleveland, Mississippi, High School) and college (Delta State University) alma maters. While coaching at Delta State in the mid-1970s, her teams won three consecutive Association for Intercollegiate Athletics for Women (AIAW) national championships and forged a 51-game winning streak.

1985

"Sneaker Wars"

On the court, Chicago Bulls rookie Michael Jordan established himself as the NBA's hot new star. He averaged 28.2 points per game on his way to winning the Rookie of the Year award. Off the court, Jordan signed an endorsement deal for a new line of Nike shoes called Air Jordans. Sports marketing, endorsement dollars, and urban fashion would never be the same.

Naming an athletic shoe after a top professional athlete ushered in the age of big-time athlete endorsements. As a pro player—particularly a basketball player—rose in fame or entered the league as a touted rookie, marketing gurus and sneaker companies engaged in fierce competition to sign him up.

Every shoe company wanted to be associated with the next big star. Over the next decade, every company from Reebok to Adidas got into the act, scrambling to sign the big names. The so-called "Sneaker Wars" had begun. By the 1990s, big-time rookies were signing endorsement contracts that were even more lucrative than their sky-high NBA salaries.

Very quickly, owning Air Jordans, or whatever the latest athlete-endorsed shoe was, became a major status symbol among American youth. Even those who could not afford the high-priced shoes felt they had to have them. This led to incidents of boys and young men being robbed for their pricey sneakers.

For Jordan, the journey from simply being a great basketball player to becoming his own worldwide marketing brand had begun.

Joe Knows Super Bowls

The AFC-champion Miami Dolphins featured record-setting quarterback Dan Marino, but the NFC-champion San Francisco 49ers had a pretty good quarterback of their own in Joe Montana when the teams met in Super Bowl XIX at Stanford Stadium in Palo Alto, California on January 20. Montana was the difference in the game, earning MVP honors after passing for three touchdowns and running for one in his team's 38–16 victory.

It was another chapter in Montana's growing football legend. He finished the day with 331 passing yards, and he was not intercepted. Running back Roger

Ty-breaking Hit *Cincinnati Reds first baseman Pete Rose singles to left field in a game in September. With the hit, his 4,192nd, Rose surpassed Ty Cobb as baseball's all-time leader (see page 54).*

Craig helped out by scoring a Super Bowl-record three touchdowns.

Meanwhile, the tough 49ers' defense swarmed all over Marino—who in the 1984 regular season became the first man to pass for more than 5,000 yards in one year—forcing him to rush passes and throw two interceptions. Marino completed 29 of his 50 passes for 318 yards, but Miami could muster little other offense.

1985

Eight Is Enough   *After losing to the Boston Celtics in all eight of their previous meetings in the NBA Finals, the Los Angeles Lakers, led by guard Earvin (Magic) Johnson, finally subdued their long-time rivals.*

Lakers Finally Beat Celtics

For the ninth time, the Boston Celtics and Los Angeles Lakers met in the NBA Finals. And for the first time, the Lakers won. Los Angeles prevailed in six games, taking the deciding game 111–100 in front of a hostile crowd at Boston Garden on June 9.

The Celtics were trying to become the first team to win back-to-back NBA championships since they did it themselves in 1967–68 and 1968–69. But this year, Magic Johnson, Kareem Abdul-Jabbar, James Worthy, and the rest of the Lakers proved too much for Larry Bird, Kevin McHale, Robert Parish, and their teammates.

Heading into the sixth game in Boston, the Lakers held a 3–2 advantage in the Finals. The Celtics were hoping to tie the series and force a seventh and deciding game—something they had never lost. But Jabbar poured in 29 points and Worthy, who averaged 23.6 points and shot 56.4 percent from the field in the series, added 28. Johnson, who averaged 18.3 points, 14 assists, and 6.8 rebounds in the series, ran the offense.

The game was tied at halftime. The Lakers opened the second half by hitting their first six shots, putting them in control, despite 32 points from McHale and 28 from Bird. What made this victory even sweeter was the fact that the Celtics had crushed the Lakers 148–114 in the series opener, setting the stage for yet another Celtics' championship. But this year, it was not to be.

Thirty-eight-year-old Jabbar, the oldest player in the NBA, was just 12 in 1959, when the Lakers' (who were based in Minneapolis at the time) Finals drought against the Celtics began.

In 1985, Jabbar was the big factor in finally shattering the Celtics' grip on the Lakers.

1985 NBA Finals

GAME	LOCATION	SCORE
1	Boston	Celtics, 148–114
2	Boston	Lakers, 109–102
3	Los Angeles	Lakers, 136–111
4	Los Angeles	Celtics, 107–105
5	Los Angeles	Lakers, 120–111
6	Boston	Lakers, 111–100

Knight's Chair Toss

Indiana University basketball coach Bobby Knight was always known as much for his hot temper as for his success on the court. During a game against University of Illinois, which Indiana lost 66–50, Knight broke a chair in a fit of rage, then made an obscene gesture at the referee—a frequent target of Knight's outbursts.

Later, in a game against Purdue University on February 23, which Indiana also lost, Knight picked up a chair and hurled it across the court, then shouted at the referee as Purdue's Steve Reid was getting ready to shoot a technical foul shot. Knight was immediately ejected from the game.

A few days later, Knight apologized, saying his action was an embarrassment to the university. He explained that he was frustrated by the officiating and lost his temper. This pattern of major tantrums and verbal abuse was repeated throughout his tenure at Indiana.

Knight's most infamous explosion occurred when he was coaching the United States team in the Pan American Games in 1979. During that tournament, Knight hit a policeman in Puerto Rico, creating an international incident. That same year, Knight threw a student newspaper photographer into the bushes because the student took his picture while he was having an argument with a bicyclist about who had the right of way.

Finally, after 29 years at Indiana, during which time he led his teams to 763 victories and three national championships, Knight was fired in September of

Magic Johnson: The First Triple Threat

Magic Johnson blurred the lines between the three positions in basketball: guard, forward, and center. He was the tallest point guard (the guard who brings the ball down the court and runs the offense) in the history of the NBA. He also excelled at forward and center. In game seven of the NBA Finals in 1980, Johnson's rookie year, he filled in at center for future Hall-of-Fame teammate Kareem Abdul-Jabbar and dominated the game, helping his team win the championship (see page 13).

Johnson quickly became the master of the triple-double—achieving double figures in points, rebounds, and assists in the same game—another demonstration of his versatility. But perhaps his biggest contribution was that he brought a team concept to the NBA at a time when most players were concentrating on their individual performances.

Johnson had enough talent to be a one-man show, but he preferred to make his teammates look good and to use his abilities to forge a winning team. His five NBA titles prove he did just that.

In 1991, Johnson's impact moved beyond the world of sports when he announced to a startled world that he had tested positive for HIV, the virus that causes AIDS. He put a familiar, trusted, beloved, celebrity face on the disease, helping to bring greater acceptance and understanding of the people who live with it.

2000 for allegedly grabbing a student by the arm because he addressed the coach as "Knight," and Knight felt that was disrespectful. In truth, it was the last straw in his long list of offenses.

Gretzky Breaks 200 Again

Wayne Gretzky broke the 200-point mark for the third time in his NHL career, scoring 73 goals and dishing out 135 assists, for a total of 208 points. He also won his unprecedented sixth consecutive MVP Award.

Most important, though, he led the Edmonton Oilers to their second straight Stanley Cup Championship, beating the Philadelphia Flyers in five games. In the deciding game on May 30, Gretzky scored a goal and had three assists in the Oilers' 8–3 victory. He got help from defenseman Paul Coffey, who added two goals.

Edmonton's Jari Kurri scored early in the first period. Thirty-five seconds later, Willie Lindstrom knocked in a shot to give the Oilers a two-goal cushion. Two more goals by Coffey in less than three minutes pushed the lead to 4–0. By the end of the second period, the Oilers were up 6–1.

Gretzky scored in the final period to finish the postseason with 47 points (17 goals, 30 assists), an NHL playoff record. The Oilers were on top again, thanks to the Great One.

Rose: All-Time Hits Leader

On September 11, Pete Rose became baseball's all-time hits leader when he picked up his 4,192nd career hit, passing legendary Hall-of-Famer Ty Cobb's career record.

Rose, who earned the nickname "Charlie Hustle," only played the game one way: hard. He pushed himself in the field, on the bases, and at bat. When the Cincinnati Reds needed a hit, there was Rose to slap the ball the other way, slashing it into the corner from either side of the plate, not bothering to slow down at first base, diving headlong into second.

With two balls and one strike on Rose, San Diego Padres pitcher Eric Show threw a fastball and Rose swung the familiar swing baseball fans had seen so many times before, and hit a clean single to left field. Baseball had a new hits leader. Rose had finally caught Cobb, who retired from baseball in 1928. In fact, Rose got his record-breaking hit 57 years to the day after Cobb's final major-league game.

Rose dashed from the batter's box, as he always did, rounding first swiftly, then scooting back to the bag. The game was stopped as flashbulbs went off all over Riverfront Stadium in Cincinnati.

Rose's 15-year-old son, Petey, reached his dad first, as players from both teams poured from the dugouts and gathered around the 44-year-old Cincinnati native. Tears streamed down his face, as he looked skyward and thought of two men who could not be there with him that day: his father, a semi-pro football player who was the biggest influence on Rose's life and his career in sports; and Cobb, whose achievement had haunted Rose through more than 20 major-league seasons.

Royals Win By Decision

The Kansas City Royals beat the St. Louis Cardinals in seven games to win a wild World Series that turned on an umpire's pivotal call in game six.

The Great One *Hockey star Wayne Gretzky celebrates after helping the Edmonton Oilers win their second consecutive Stanley Cup.*

Kansas City had reached the Series in dramatic fashion. First, the Royals edged the California Angels to win the American League West by a single game. Then, they rallied from a three games to one deficit by winning three consecutive games and beating the Toronto Blue Jays in seven games in the American League Championship Series (ALCS).

In the National League, the Cardinals won a big-league-best 101 games in the regular season, then qualified for the Fall Classic when Jack Clark belted a three-run home run in the ninth inning to win the sixth, and final, game of the National

League Championship Series (NLCS) against the Los Angeles Dodgers.

The drama carried over to the World Series. St. Louis won a taut opening game, then scored four times in the ninth inning of game two to rally for a 4–2 victory and take a commanding lead in the Series. The Cardinals still held a three-games-to-two lead and were three outs away from a championship when they carried a 1–0 lead into the bottom of the ninth inning of game six at Kansas City.

Frontier Woman *Libby Riddles became the first woman to win the grueling Iditarod Sled Dog Race.*

Pinch-hitter Jorge Orta led off the ninth inning for the Royals and quickly fell behind no balls and two strikes. Then he grounded to Clark at first base, who threw to pitcher Todd Worrell covering for an apparent out. But umpire Don Denkinger ruled Orta safe—though television replays clearly indicated it was the wrong call. The Cardinals then came unglued. Clark misplayed a foul pop that should have been caught, and a single, a passed ball, and Dane Iorg's single won the game for the Royals, 2–1.

Game seven the next night was no contest. The Royals scored twice in the second inning and three more times in the third to open a 5–0 advantage. In the fifth, the Cardinals lost their composure. Pitcher Joaquin Andujar was ejected during a six-run outburst by the Royals, who went on to win 11–0.

Dominant "D"

The Chicago Bears wreaked havoc on the NFL in 1985 with an intimidating defense that turned in one of the most dominating performances of all time. Head coach Mike Ditka's Bears rolled to 15 wins in 16 games during the regular season, then outscored three postseason opponents by a combined 91–10 to win their ninth NFL championship, but their first of the Super Bowl era.

The success of the 1985 Bears was tied to the 46 Defense. Defensive coordinator Buddy Ryan crowded eight players near the line of scrimmage and confounded opposing offenses with pressure from multiple areas. Ryan installed the 46 in 1981, but it wasn't 1985 that the unit

Other Milestones of 1985

✔ The 45-second shot clock was added to college basketball to help speed up the game.

✔ On July 11, Nolan Ryan became the first pitcher in baseball history to strike out 4,000 batters. Ryan was just getting warmed up, though. By the time he retired following the 1993 season, he had a record 5,714 career strikeouts.

✔ Future Hall-of-Fame pitcher Tom Seaver won his 300th game on August 4 for the Chicago White Sox, becoming only the 17th player in Major League Baseball history to do so.

Eddie Robinson

✔ On August 21, Mary Decker set a new women's record, running the mile in 4 minutes, 16.71 seconds. She broke the old mark of 4 minutes, 17.44 seconds by Maricica Puica of Romania.

✔ Grambling State University football coach Eddie Robinson passed Paul "Bear" Bryant, with his 324th victory on November 23, to become the winningest coach in the history of college football.

✔ The North American Soccer League, the latest unsuccessful attempt at a pro soccer league in the United States, suspended operations after 18 years.

---

achieved near perfection. That season, the Bears' opponents managed a meager 12.4 points per game during the regular season. Chicago allowed 10 or fewer points in 14 of 19 games (including postseason).

By the way, the name of the 46 had nothing to do with the way the players lined up. Instead, it was the uniform number of Doug Plank, a hard-hitting safety who was one of the keys to Ryan's original innovative defense in the early 1980s. By 1985, however, Plank was out of the league, having retired after playing in only one game in 1982.

In the 2009 season, Plank became an assistant on the New York Jets' staff of rookie head coach Rex Ryan, the son of Buddy Ryan.

Women's Pioneer

The Women's Sports Foundation named Libby Riddles its Professional Sportswoman of the Year for 1985. Riddles had made history earlier in the year, on March 20, when she became the first woman ever to win the Iditarod Sled Dog Race in Alaska.

The Iditarod is a grueling test of endurance in which competitors guide a team of dogs more than 1,050 miles through beautiful, but rugged, terrain that includes mountain ranges, rivers, and forest, often in the harshest weather. Riddles, in fact, had to navigate through a deadly blizzard across Norton Sound en route to her victory.

1986

Baseball Suspends Seven

Drug use continued to invade the world of sports—this time Major League Baseball. Baseball commissioner Peter Ueberroth handed out one-year suspensions to seven players, saying that they had used drugs themselves or aided in spreading drugs within baseball.

Keith Hernandez (New York Mets), Dale Berra (New York Yankees), Joaquin Andujar (Oakland Athletics), Dave Parker (Cincinnati Reds), Jeffrey Leonard (San Francisco Giants), Lonnie Smith (Kansas City Royals), and Enos Cabell (Los Angeles Dodgers) were all suspended without pay.

All seven players chose an alternative penalty offered by Ueberroth, which resulted in the lifting of the suspensions. The players agreed to give 10 percent of their salaries for the 1986 season to drug-prevention programs and to put in up to 200 hours of community service over the next two years. They also agreed to undergo drug tests for the remainder of their major-league careers.

The players either testified or were implicated during the 1985 investigations and trials of seven men charged with distributing cocaine. Although none of the players was charged in those trials, six of the seven gave incriminating testimony. The seventh, Andujar, was named by several players as a cocaine user.

In an attempt to stem the spreading tide of drug use, Ueberroth also gave out lesser penalties to 14 other players.

Celtics Back on Top

Forward Larry Bird posted a "triple-double," scoring 29 points, grabbing 11 rebounds, and handing out 12 assists to lead the Boston Celtics to a 114–97 win over the Houston Rockets in the sixth, and deciding, game of the NBA Finals on June 8 at the Boston Garden. The championship was the Celtics' second in three seasons, and their record 16th overall.

During the regular season, Bird ranked among the league leaders in scoring (25.8 points per game), rebounding (9.8 rebounds per game), steals (2.02 steals per game), free-throw percentage (89.6 percent), and three-point-field-goal percentage (42.3 percent). He won his third straight NBA Most Valuable Player award, joining former Celtics' great Bill Russell and former Celtics' archrival Wilt

Celtic Pride   *Forward Larry Bird (33) and Celtics brought another NBA championship to Boston.*

Chamberlain as the only players in NBA history to win the award three years in a row. And he helped Boston take back the NBA championship.

One of the main reason's for Bird's and the Celtics' success was a trade that brought veteran center Bill Walton to Boston. This gave the Celtics' already strong front court of Bird, Kevin McHale, and Robert Parish another top scorer, passer,

rebounder, and defender. The addition of Walton also gave Parish some much-needed rest at center. Walton was an unselfish and team-oriented player—much like Bird. When the two were on the court together, the ball seemed to fly everywhere, always eventually finding an open man.

In the regular season the team won 67 games, the most ever for the famous

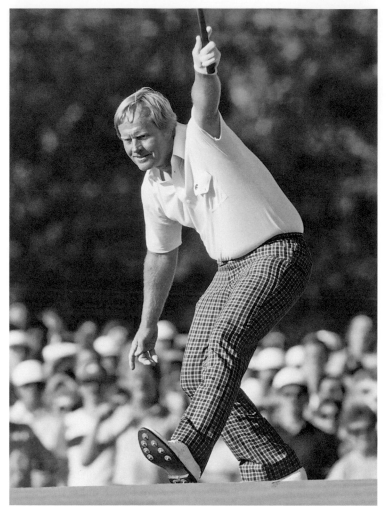

Watch the Birdie! *Jack Nicklaus starts to celebrate as his putt drops for a crucial birdie on the 17th hole of the final round of the Masters golf tournament. At 46, Nicklaus won the title for the sixth time.*

Major Achievement

Jack Nicklaus watched intently as his 18-foot putt rolled toward the 17th hole during the final round of the Masters at the Augusta National Golf Club on April 13. As the putt neared the hole, Nicklaus raised his club in triumph. "Yes, sir!" announcer Verne Lundquist exclaimed to a national television audience. Nicklaus, the greatest golfer of his (and perhaps, any) generation, had just taken the lead in one of golf's most prestigious tournaments.

Nicklaus went on to close out a final-round 65—he shot an incredible six-under-par 30 on the back nine—to edge Tom Kite and Greg Norman by one shot and win the tournament.

At 46, Nicklaus became the oldest man ever to win one of golf's major championships (now defined as the Masters, U.S. Open, British Open, and PGA Championship). It was his record sixth green jacket as the winner of the Masters, and his 18th major championship in all (another record).

Star Dies From Cocaine

Twenty-two year old Len Bias, an All-American basketball star at the University of Maryland, died on June 19 from using cocaine—just two days after being selected by the Boston Celtics as the number-two pick in the NBA draft.

The 6-foot-8 Bias was Maryland's all-time leading scorer, with 2,149 points during his college career. He averaged 23.3 points per game, pulled down 224 rebounds, and was voted the Atlantic Coast

Celtics. At home, they were nearly unbeatable, posting a regular-season record of 40–1 at the Boston Garden. Then they went 10–0 at home in the playoffs.

The Rockets, led by a pair of seven-footers—Ralph Sampson and Hakeem Olajuwon—beat the defending-champion Los Angeles Lakers in the final round of the Western Conference playoffs but were no match for Boston in the NBA Finals.

Conference's Player of the Year during his final season.

After an exciting day in Boston, during which Bias was introduced as the Celtics' next great star, Bias returned to the Maryland campus. The following night, he was with two teammates when he died suddenly. Autopsy reports showed that he died of intoxication from cocaine, which he most likely snorted only minutes before his death. The sports world was shocked at the tragic loss of a young life and a potential NBA great.

USFL Closes Shop

After three years as a professional football league, trying to compete with the NFL for players and fans, the United States Football League (USFL) disbanded, calling off its 1986 season.

The league began in 1983 with 12 teams, and for three years had played a spring schedule to avoid going head-to-head with the NFL's fall games. But in 1986, the USFL decided to switch to a fall schedule and compete directly with the older league.

After trying unsuccessfully to get a television contract—a must for the survival of any professional sports league—the USFL filed a lawsuit against the NFL, claiming that it monopolized the television networks and prevented the younger league from getting a contract to broadcast their games. The USFL asked for more than $1 billion in damages.

Following a long trial, a jury ruled that although the NFL was a professional monopoly, it had done nothing to keep the USFL off the air. That decision had been made by the networks themselves. Damages were awarded to the USFL in the amount of $1.

Without big money from the lawsuit or a television contract, USFL team owners felt they could not continue operating. The league had already lost more than $150 million in its first three seasons. Six days after the suit ended, the league's remaining eight teams voted to cease operations.

Running back Herschel Walker, the USFL's biggest star and greatest hope for

Bird Flies

At a time in the NBA when high-flying schoolyard moves and flashy slam dunks were the norm, forward Larry Bird stepped onto the parquet floor at the Boston Garden and did something that had not been seen in the league in awhile. He made his teammates better.

After a stunning college career at Indiana State University, capped by a college player of the year award in his senior year and a memorable showdown in the NCAA championship game against Magic Johnson's Michigan State team (won by Johnson and Michigan State), Bird joined the Boston Celtics.

The once-great NBA dynasty was struggling through a low period. In his rookie season, Bird led his team to 32 more victories than the previous year. He went on to win three NBA championships, three consecutive Most Valuable Player awards, and, along with Magic Johnson, reinvigorate interest in the NBA.

After playing with the United States Olympic "Dream Team" in Barcelona, Spain in 1992, Bird retired as a player, due to a bad back. He went on to become a successful professional coach with the Indiana Pacers. In 1998, he was enshrined in basketball's Hall of Fame.

1986

success, signed a five-year contract with the NFL's Dallas Cowboys. In 1989, he was the centerpiece in the largest trade in NFL history, when he was dealt to the Minnesota Vikings as part of a deal involving 18 players or draft picks.

Joyner Sets Record

Jackie Joyner (b.1962), who won the silver medal in the heptathlon at the 1984 Olympics and went on to take the gold in the event in 1988, set a new world record in the heptathlon at the Goodwill Games in Moscow on July 7, smashing individual event records along the way.

Closing Time *The United States Football League made a splash by signing big-name stars such as Herschel Walker (34), but too many empty seats spelled its doom. The league folded in 1986 (see page 61).*

Joyner totaled 7,148 points, becoming the first woman to break the 7,000-point mark in the grueling seven-event competition, and beating the record set by Sabine Paetz of East Germany in 1984 by 202 points.

The heptathlon is a two-day competition made up of seven events: the 100-meter hurdles, the shot put, the high jump, the 200-meter race, the long jump, the javelin, and the 800-meter race.

Joyner set a first-day record by scoring 4,151 points in four events. She ran the 100-meter hurdles in 12.85 seconds, a new American heptathlon record. Then she leaped 62 inches in the high jump; threw the shot put 48 feet, 5 1/4 inches; and ran the 200 meters in 23 seconds.

The second day of competition began with Joyner setting a heptathlon world record by jumping 23 feet in the long jump, her favorite event. She then tossed the javelin 163 feet, 4 inches.

In the final event, Joyner ran the 800-meter race in 2 minutes, 10.02 seconds to capture the heptathlon record. Despite the United States' boycott of the Olympics in Moscow in 1980 and the Soviet boycott of the Games in Los Angeles in 1984, the American was cheered wildly by Goodwill Games fans in Moscow as she set the new standard in her sport.

One Strike Away

The 1986 Major League Baseball playoffs—the American League Championship Series (ALCS), the National League Championship Series (NLCS), and the World Series—were among the most exciting and memorable in baseball history.

Boston Red Sox fans cheered their team to a great regular season, but October 12 they appeared to once again be watching their beloved Sox get eliminated in the postseason. The California Angels led the ALCS three games to one, and led game five by a score of 5–4 in the top of the ninth inning.

Boston centerfielder Dave Henderson, faced the Angels' top relief pitcher, Donnie Moore. Henderson worked the count to two balls and two strikes, then drove a pitch into the stands in left field for a two-run homer that gave Boston the lead, 6–5. Although the Angels came back to tie the game in the bottom of the ninth inning, the Red Sox scored again in the11th inning to win 7–6.

The Angels never recovered. Boston won the next two games easily to earn a spot in the October Series.

Meanwhile, in the NLCS, the New York Mets battled the Houston Astros, who were led by pitcher Mike Scott. Scott won 18 games during the regular season while leading the league with 306 strikeouts and a 2.22 earned run average (ERA—the average number of runs charged to the pitcher per nine innings). He was named the National League Cy Young Award winner and the NLCS Most Valuable Player in 1985, despite the fact that his team lost the playoff series.

Scott dominated the Mets, shutting them out 1–0 in game one, then taking a 3–1 victory in game four. Heading into game six in Houston on October 15, the Mets led the series three games to two. If they lost game six, they would have to face Scott again in a deciding game seven—a fate they were hoping to avoid.

No Rush Hour in New York

Game six of the NLCS began at 3:06 p.m. New York time, and finally ended at 7:48. There was no rush hour in usually busy New York City that night, as office workers stayed in their offices to catch the end of this seemingly endless game.

Buses and subways were half empty, though announcements at Grand Central Station kept the few commuters who did head home updated on the score. People on the street gathered around anyone who had a radio or huddled outside the windows of appliance stores that had TV sets on, unable to leave for fear of missing the latest twist or turn.

The great city slowed down to linger and learn the fate of its beloved Mets.

The Astros jumped out to a 3–0 lead in the first inning, then Houston pitcher Bob Knepper shut down the Mets for eight innings. New York finally scored three times in the top of the ninth to tie the game and send it into extra innings.

The Mets scored a run in the top of the 14th inning, but Houston tied it in the bottom of the 14th. Then, in the top of the 16th inning, New York scored three runs to grab what seemed to be a commanding 7–4 lead. Houston came back to score two in the bottom of the 16th, and had the tying run on second base when Mets relief pitcher Jesse Orosco struck out Houston rightfielder Kevin Bass to end the marathon and send the Mets to the World Series.

But the exciting ALCS and NLCS were only prelude to the astounding World Series still to come.

The Red Sox won the first two games in New York, then the Mets returned the favor, taking the next two in Boston. The Red Sox jumped out to a three-games-to-two lead, winning game five 4–2 in Boston.

1986

The series returned to New York for game six on October 25, with the Red Sox one win away from capturing their first World Series since 1918. The game was tied 3–3 after nine innings, but Boston took the lead in the top of the 10th, scoring two runs.

The first two Mets to bat in the bottom of the 10th inning were easily retired by Boston relief pitcher Calvin Schiraldi. Then Gary Carter and Kevin Mitchell both hit singles. The next batter, Ray Knight, fell behind in the count 0–2. Just as they were one strike away from elimination in the ALCS, the Red Sox were now one strike away from winning the World Series.

Knight singled to center, scoring Carter and cutting the Boston lead to 5–4. Mitchell moved to third base. The Red Sox brought in a new pitcher, Bob Stanley, to face Mookie Wilson.

Wilson worked the count to 2–2, and once again Boston was one strike away from victory. But Wilson kept fouling off pitches. Stanley's seventh pitch was wild, scoring Mitchell from third and tying the game at 5–5.

Three pitches later, Wilson hit a ground ball that dribbled through the legs of Boston first baseman Bill Buckner, scoring Knight with the winning run, setting off a wild celebration among the Mets' players, and tying the Series at three games apiece.

The 36-year-old Buckner normally would have been removed from the game in favor of a defensive replacement. But he had played such an important role in the Red Sox's success that Boston manager John McNamara left him in the game so he could enjoy the presumed victory celebration.

Stunned, the Red Sox lost game seven by a score of 8–5 and the Mets won the World Series, capping off an unforgettable postseason.

An American in Paris *Greg LeMond became the first man from the United States to win the Tour de France, cycling's most important event and one of the most famous athletic competitions in the world.*

Sports Marketing Grows

As a direct result of the increasing connection between professional sports and athlete-endorsed products, sneaker manufacturer Nike topped the billion-dollar mark in revenue for the first time in its history.

Other Milestones of 1986

✔ Following their overwhelming 46–10 victory against the New England Patriots in Super Bowl XX on January 26, the Chicago Bears made the first sports music video, "The Super Bowl Shuffle."

✔ On February 8, Debi Thomas became the first African-American figure skater to win the world championship.

✔ Bill James published his *Historical Baseball Abstract*, a groundbreaking book with insightful statistical analysis.

✔ Boston Red Sox pitcher Roger Clemens struck out 20 Seattle Mariners' batters during his team's 3–1 victory at Fenway Park on April 29, setting a new single-game record (a decade later, in 1996, Clemens tied his own mark by striking out 20 Detroit Tigers in a game). The old mark of 19 was held by four

Mike Tyson

players. Clemens also won both the Cy Young and AL MVP awards in 1986.

✔ Nancy Lieberman became the first woman to play in a men's basketball league when she joined the United States Basketball League's Springfield Fame.

✔ The three-point field goal was introduced in college basketball.

✔ The NFL approved the use of instant replay as a tool to aid officials, who could reverse their decisions on certain calls after reviewing visual evidence.

✔ Wayne Gretzky scored his 500th goal on November 22 while breaking his single-season scoring record of 212 points; he racked up 214 points.

✔ Also on November 22, 20-year-old boxer Mike Tyson knocked out Trevor Berbick to become the youngest heavyweight boxing champion in history.

Nike, makers of the famous Air Jordan basketball shoe, extended its product line and its enormous sports marketing reach beyond sneakers and into the apparel business. The company introduced clothing collections endorsed by NBA star Michael Jordan and tennis great John McEnroe.

American Wins in France

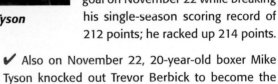 It is considered by many to be the largest, most important, and most difficult sporting event in the world. The Tour de France is a grueling 21-day bicycle race in which cyclists ride between 100 and 150 miles each day, often up steep and winding mountain roads.

On July 27, Greg LeMond, a 25-year-old who was born in 1961 in Los Angeles, California, became the first American to win this contest of strength, endurance, skill, and willpower. Battling teammate Bernard Hinault, LeMond pedaled triumphantly into Paris and became an immediate media celebrity and American sports hero.

1987

Simms Leads Giants

The New York Giants rallied in the second half to defeat the Denver Broncos 39–20 in Super Bowl XXI on January 25 in Pasadena, California. It was the Giants' first Super Bowl victory (in their first appearance) and sent the Broncos to the first of their three Super Bowl losses in a four-season span.

New York trailed 10–9 at halftime, but rode the pinpoint passing of game MVP Phil Simms to win. For the game, Simms completed 22 of his 25 passes for 268 yards and three touchdowns. His completion rate of 88 percent remains a Super Bowl record (entering 2010).

After tough defense dominated the first two quarters, Simms tossed a 13-yard touchdown pass to Mark Bavaro early in the third quarter. He then led the Giants down the field for a short field goal, followed by another drive capped by Joe Morris' one-yard touchdown run. Simms also threw a six-yard touchdown pass to Phil McConkey in the fourth quarter, putting the game out of reach at 33–10.

Denver quarterback John Elway passed for 304 yards, but much of it came with the game out of hand.

Sugar Ray Is Back

In 1982, welterweight boxing champion Sugar Ray Leonard retired due to a detached retina in his left eye. Doctors told him that if he kept boxing, there was a chance he could lose vision in the eye.

On April 6, Leonard came out of retirement to battle World Boxing Council (WBC) middleweight champion Marvelous Marvin Hagler. The time away did not seem to diminish Leonard's great boxing skills. He danced, spun, and jabbed his way through the first few rounds, then stood toe-to-toe with Hagler, outslugging the champ as the fight drew to a close.

When it was over, the scores were close, but Leonard took a 12-round, split decision to capture the middleweight title. The more than 15,000 fans in the Las Vegas arena chanted his name, as Leonard earned his 34th victory in 35 fights. Hagler's record was 63–3, with 52 knockouts.

Dodger VP Resigns

Seventy-year-old Al Campanis (1916–1998), vice president in charge of player personnel for baseball's Los Angeles Dodgers, resigned on April 8, fol-

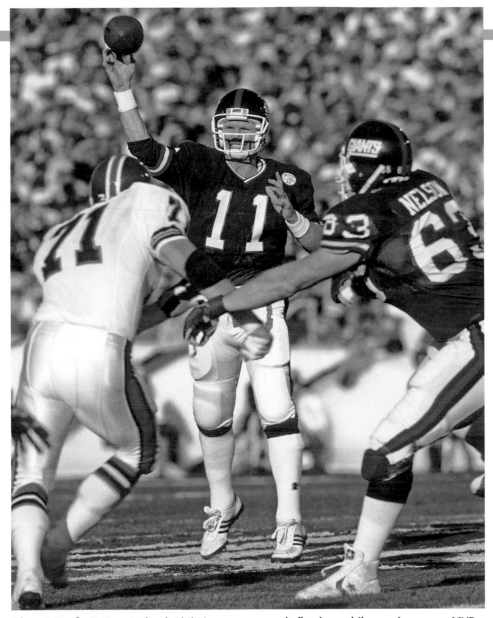

Almost Perfect *Quarterback Phil Simms was nearly flawless while earning game MVP honors in the New York Giants' victory over the Denver Broncos in Super Bowl XXI.*

lowing national outrage over remarks he made on the ABC television show *Nightline* two days earlier.

Campanis appeared on the show, hosted by Ted Koppel, to help celebrate the 40th anniversary of Jackie Robinson breaking baseball's color barrier. Koppel asked Campanis why he thought the major leagues had no black managers, general managers, or owners. Campanis

1987

replied, "I truly believe that they may not have some of the necessities to be, let's say, a field manager, or perhaps a GM."

When Koppel asked him if he really believed that, the Dodgers' vice president said, "Well, I don't say all of them, but they are short. How many quarterbacks do you have, how many pitchers do you have, that are black?" Then Campanis added, "Why are black men or black people not good swimmers? Because they don't have any buoyancy."

These comments set off a storm of controversy, forcing Campanis to apologize.

He claimed that his statements were taken the wrong way and that he did not think blacks are less intelligent than whites. Two days after the remarks, however, Campanis resigned from the Dodgers.

He had been with the Dodgers' organization for 46 years, including seven games as a player in 1943. After serving in World War II, Campanis worked as a manager in the Dodgers' minor-league system. He became a scout in 1950 and director of scouting from 1957 to 1968, before finally settling in as a club vice president in 1969.

Queen of the Iditarod

In March, Susan Butcher won the Iditarod dogsled race. The Iditarod is one of the few sporting events in which men and women compete straight up against each other. Butcher not only beat out the 61 men and 1 other woman in the 1987 race, but she also did it in record time: In finishing in 11 days, 2 hours, 5 minutes, and 13 seconds, she shattered the old record by 13 hours.

This was the second year in a row that Butcher won the grueling, 1,150-mile race through the snowy Alaskan wilderness, and she went on to win it again in 1988. After placing second in 1989, she returned to the top in 1990. Her four wins in five years made it the most dominant stretch for any dogsled driver in Iditarod history.

Butcher was not the first woman to win the Iditarod. That honor belonged to Libby Riddles in 1985 (see page 57). Together, their success helped spur T-shirt slogans such as, "Alaska: Where Men Are Men and Women Win the Iditarod."

In 2002, Butcher was faced with her biggest challenge yet when she faced a severe blood disorder that eventually was diagnosed as leukemia. She fought the disease with the same determination and toughness that characterized her performances in the Iditarod. In August of 2006, though, she died. She was 51.

Since 2008, Alaskans have celebrated Susan Butcher Day on the first Saturday of March. Traditionally, that's also the day the annual Iditarod starts.

Susan Butcher

He had actually played as a minor leaguer with Robinson 41 years earlier, and helped to sign minority players such as Roberto Clemente and Tommy Davis, but his questionable comments on Nightline spelled the end of his lengthy baseball career.

Amazing Streak Ends

The most incredible winning streak in the history of track events finally came to an end 10 years after it had begun. Between 1977 and 1987, Edwin Moses won 122 consecutive races in the 400-meter intermediate hurdles (400 IM), setting what may be an unbeatable record.

In 1976, Moses won a gold medal in the event at the Munich, West Germany Olympics. The follow year, after a loss to West German Harald Schmid, his amazing winning streak began. As the streak grew longer, Moses took a track event that had lacked glamour and didn't get much attention, and brought it into the spotlight. Along the way, he became one of the sport's biggest stars.

For 10 years, there was no one even in the same class as Moses, who won another Olympic gold medal in 1984 (he didn't have a chance in 1980 because of the United States' boycott of the Games). He set the world record in the 400 IM at 47.02 seconds, and he also owns the next 10 fastest times in the event.

The mental attitude Moses brought to each of the 122 races was as big a factor in his success as his extraordinary physical ability. "The day I feel nice and relaxed," Moses said in 1984, "is the day I'll know the streak is in danger."

All Four Won   *Al Unser, Sr. won the Indianapolis 500 at the "Brickyard," the Indianapolis Motor Speedway. Unser joined A.J. Foyt as the only four-time winners of the world-renowned race (see page 70).*

Three years later, on June 4, 21-year-old American hurdler Danny Harris finally defeated the 31-year-old Moses in a 400 IM race. Harris took the lead at the fifth hurdle and finished with a time of 47.56 seconds. Moses finished right behind him, with a time of 47.69 seconds.

The crowd of 11,000 in Madrid, Spain, stood and chanted Moses' name as he ran a solo lap of honor around the track to celebrate his astounding streak.

1987

Unser Wins Fourth 500

 Al Unser, Sr., became the second driver in history to win the Indianapolis 500 four times when he captured the world's most prestigious motor race on May 24, winning by a margin of just five seconds. At age 47, Unser also became the oldest driver to win the race.

His previous victories came in 1970, 1971, and 1978. His four wins at Indy tied the record set by A.J. Foyt. Unser's 25-year-old son, Al Unser, Jr., finished fourth in the race.

The senior Unser averaged 162.175 miles per hour in front of the crowd of 400,000 racing fans at the Indianapolis Motor Speedway. The veteran drove in third place for most of the race, with Mario Andretti in the lead for 170 of the

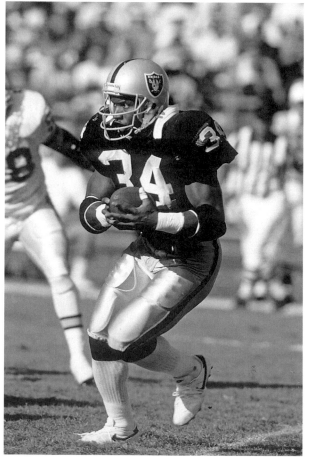

Bo Knows Baseball . . . and Bo Knows Football *Bo Jackson already was a star for baseball's Kansas City Royals when he also signed to play football for the NFL's Los Angeles Raiders. He excelled at both sports.*

200 laps, and Roberto Guerrero in second place, where he finished the race just seconds behind Unser.

During lap number 180, Andretti's engine failed, pulling him out of the race. Guerrero then made a rookie mistake during a pit stop that cost him an extra 55 seconds—enough to allow Unser to take the lead and eventually the race.

Gretzky Leads Oilers

Wayne Gretzky won his unprecedented eighth consecutive Hart Memorial Trophy, the award given annually to the NHL's most valuable player. By decade's end he had won the award nine of 10 years. Gretzky also led his Edmonton Oilers to the Stanley Cup, the team's third NHL championship in four years.

In a well-played, seven-game final series, the Great One had some help in game seven to lock up the cup. Teammates Jari Kurri and Glen Anderson put the Oilers in the lead to stay with second- and third-period goals, respectively, as Edmonton beat the Philadelphia Flyers 3–1 on May 31 to capture the series. The Oilers' superb defensive play helped seal the victory.

Philadelphia goalie Ron Hextall had kept the underdog Flyers alive in the series with outstanding performances after the Oilers jumped out to a three-games-to-one lead. Led by Hextall's excellent goaltending, the Flyers bounced back to win game five 4–3 and game six 3–2 to tie the series, setting up the decisive seventh game.

In game seven, Hextall didn't get much help from his teammates, as he dealt with 43 Oilers' shots on goal, compared to only 20 shots faced by Edmonton goalie Grant Fuhr.

Bo Plays Two Pro Sports

Calling it a "hobby" to get him through the winter, pro baseball player Bo Jackson signed a five-year contract to play pro football with the Los Angeles Raiders. Jackson was already playing Major League Baseball for the Kansas City Royals. The agreement called for Jackson to join the Raiders at the end of the baseball season, which would allow him to play in about half of the team's 16 NFL games.

While at Auburn University in 1985, Jackson won the Heisman Trophy as college football's best player. The following spring, he was the number-one overall pick in the NFL draft but turned down a

Two-Sport Superstar

By the time Bo Jackson—the 1985 Heisman Trophy winner as college football's top player—signed his first pro football contract, he had already established himself as an amazingly talented Major League Baseball player. He hit massive home runs nearing 500 feet in distance, made impossible throws from the deepest parts of ballparks, and climbed outfield walls to haul in long fly balls and take back home runs.

During the years that he played both professional sports, from 1987 through 1990, Jackson emerged as one of the most feared hitters in baseball and one of the fastest and most unstoppable running backs in the NFL.

A serious hip injury in 1991 ended his football career and cut short his baseball career. Others have played two sports, but no one has shown such ability in both.

1987

lucrative offer from the Tampa Bay Buccaneers. Instead, Jackson signed a deal with baseball's Royals and played with one of their minor-league teams.

His first full season in Major League Baseball was 1987. At the time he signed with the football Raiders—during baseball's All-Star break in July—Jackson was batting .254, with 18 homers and 45 RBI.

NFL Strike. . . Again

The National Football League Players Association went on strike two games into the 1987 season. The NFL players last staged a strike in 1982, when they shut down the game for 57 days (see page 33). This time, the players were hoping to gain unrestricted free agency—the

Other Milestones of 1987

✔ On January 2, head coach Joe Paterno's Penn State Nittany Lions won college football's national championship for the 1986 season by beating the top-ranked Miami Hurricanes 14–10 in the Fiesta Bowl in Tempe, Arizona.

✔ Three years after losing the America's Cup to Australia, an American skipper, Dennis Conner, regained it on February 4, sailing the ship *Stars & Stripes*.

✔ Woody Hayes, longtime football coaching great at Ohio State University, died on March 12 at age 74.

✔ Philadelphia Phillies third baseman Mike Schmidt hit his 500th career home run on April 18, joining baseball's most elite group of sluggers.

✔ The Atlanta Braves started baseball's trend away from the pullover polyester uniforms of the 1970s and early '80s, going back to traditional button-up jerseys and returning to the team logo they had used 25 years earlier in Milwaukee.

Dennis Conner

✔ Julius Erving joined Wilt Chamberlain and Kareem Abdul-Jabbar as the only players in NBA history to score more than 30,000 career points.

✔ The Little League World Series celebrated its 40th anniversary in August.

✔ Magic Johnson was the NBA playoff MVP, leading the Los Angeles Lakers to their fourth title in eight years over the Boston Celtics.

✔ Two years after his Cy Young Award performance, New York Mets pitcher Dwight Gooden tested positive for drugs and entered a rehabilitation program.

✔ Mark McGwire of the Oakland Athletics set a record for baseball rookies with 49 home runs in his first season.

✔ On the title track of Public Enemy's debut album, "Yo! Bum Rush the Show," Chuck D rapped about the Chicago Bears' victory over the New England Patriots in Super Bowl XX.

right to sign with any team when a contract was up. They were also looking for a higher salary scale and increased pension benefits, as well as some minor contractual points.

The NFL responded by hiring replacement players. Games scheduled for the third weekend of the season were canceled, but the games in weeks four, five, and six were played with the replacement players.

The 24-day strike ended on October 15, and striking players returned for the seventh week of the season without a new contract, a back-to-work agreement, or a new collective bargaining agreement in place. Although some agreements were reached on minor issues, the major questions of free agency, drug testing, and pension funding were left unresolved.

One Catch, Two Records

San Francisco 49ers wide receiver Jerry Rice set two NFL records with a single pass reception, catching a 20-yard touchdown pass from quarterback Steve Young in the third quarter of a game against the Atlanta Falcons on December 20.

The reception, Rice's 19th of the year, broke the record for the most touchdown catches in a season. It also marked the 12th consecutive game in which Rice had caught a touchdown pass, another NFL record.

By season's end, Rice had 22 touchdown receptions—a remarkable figure, especially given that he reached it in only 12 games because of the players' strike early in the year. But Rice, who was in his third NFL season after being selected in the first round of the 1985 draft, was just getting started. He would go on to become the most prolific touchdown scorer the league has ever known.

Rice played for the 49ers through the 2000 season, then joined the Oakland Raiders in 2001. He helped the Raiders reach the Super Bowl in the 2002 season, then played one more full season in Oakland and part of another before closing his career with the Seattle Seahawks in 2004.

In 20 NFL seasons, Rice caught 1,549 passes for 22,895 yards and 197 touchdowns. All of those are league records—and all by a very wide margin. His 207 total touchdowns is another league mark.

1988

Golden Winter Olympics

At the 1988 Winter Olympics in Calgary, Canada in February—the first Olympic Games of the decade without a boycott of some kind—the United States came away with two gold medals. Both of these medals were hard fought, and both required near-perfect performances.

In men's figure skating, American Brian Boitano captured the gold medal in one of the closest competitions in Olympic history. Boitano beat Canadian Brian Orser by a slim margin, as the Canadian took the silver. Viktor Petrenko of the Soviet Union won the bronze. Boitano had a very narrow lead after the short program, leaving plenty of room for Orser to overtake him. But the American skated with great skill, showmanship, and emotion, delivering a stunning performance in the long program to secure his gold medal.

America's other gold came in women's speed skating. Bonnie Blair set a world record in the 500-meter sprint, capturing the gold with a time of 39.10 seconds. Blair knew she would have to skate a world's best time to win, having watched defending Olympic champion Christa Rothenburger of East Germany break her own world record just moments earlier in the competition. Rothenburger set the new record at 39.12 seconds. With that in mind, Blair skated to the gold, shaving Rothenburger's time by just two one-hundredths of a second.

Lakers Repeat NBA Title

In an exciting, seven-game NBA Finals, the Los Angeles Lakers edged the Detroit Pistons to win the league championship for the fifth time in the 1980s and for the 12th time overall. The Lakers won the decisive game 108–105 in Los Angeles on June 21.

The Lakers' title also marked the first time since 1969 that an NBA team successfully defended its league crown. (Boston won consecutive championships in 1967–68 and 1968–69.) After his team's victory in the 1987 NBA Finals over the Celtics, Lakers coach Pat Riley was asked if his team could win again the following year. "I'll guarantee it," Riley replied.

His team proved to be as good as his word. The Lakers had home-court advantage throughout the playoffs, thanks to a league-best 62–20 regular-season record, and they certainly needed it. Each of their

Close Call *Brian Boitano won gold at the Winter Games by the slimmest of margins.*

other series—hard fought contests against the Utah Jazz and Dallas Mavericks—also came down to a deciding seventh game on their home court.

James Worthy led the way in game seven of the finals with the first triple-double (double figures in points, assists, and rebounds) of his career: 36 points, 16 rebounds, and 10 assists.

Night Games at Wrigley

For 74 years, the Chicago Cubs played by day—the way the game was intended to be played, at least according to purists. Only day games were played at Wrigley Field, the Cubs' home stadium (they also played on real grass, not artificial turf). But on August 9, Wrigley Field

1988

became the last Major League Baseball stadium to get lights, and night games could finally be played.

The 36,399 fans on hand were filled with mixed emotions, happy to be a part of history, but sad at the end of a proud tradition. The Cubs beat the New York Mets 6–4 in the first official Wrigley night game. The ceremony introducing the lights actually took place the night before, on August 8, as a 91-year-old Cubs fan flipped a switch to turn on the 540 lights that had been placed on the stadium's roof. But the game that night against the Philadelphia Phillies lasted only three and a half innings before it was postponed by rain.

After years of debate, the decision to put lights into Wrigley Field was finalized earlier in the year. The Cubs' management gave in to the economic reality that the franchise could fill the stands with bigger crowds for night games. However, only 18 night games were scheduled for the 1988 season.

Dodgers Feats

The Los Angeles Dodgers' Orel Hershiser and Kirk Gibson turned in two of the most memorable individual performances in baseball history in 1988. It was only fitting, then, that the Dodgers won the World Series, beating the favored Oakland Athletics in five games. The decisive game was a 5–2 victory in Oakland on October 20.

Hershiser, a right-handed pitcher, set a big-league record for consecutive shutout innings. In his final start of the regular season on September 28, Hershiser threw 10 shutout innings, bringing his streak of consecutive scoreless innings to 59 and breaking the record set by Dodgers great Don Drysdale in 1968. Hershiser, who was just about unhittable over the final month of the season, won 23 games in all and captured the National League Cy Young Award.

Hershiser continued his dominance into the postseason. On October 12, he shut out the New York Mets 6–0 in the seventh and deciding game of the National League Championship Series, propelling the Dodgers into the World Series.

In the World Series, Hershiser won two games, including another shutout in game two, then a complete-game victory in the deciding game five.

Hershiser shared World Series heroics with teammate Gibson. In game one of the Series at Dodger Stadium, the Dodgers trailed 4–3 with two outs in the bottom

59 Shutout Innings

Here is how Orel Hershiser set a record for consecutive scoreless innings in 1988:

OPPONENT	SCORE	SCORELESS INNINGS PITCHED
Montreal Expos	4–2	4
Atlanta Braves	3–0	9
Cincinnati Reds	5–0	9
Atlanta Braves	1–0	9
Houston Astros	1–0	9
San Francisco Giants	3–0	9
San Diego Padres	0–0 *	10
Total		59

*Hershiser left the game after 10 innings with the score 0–0. The Dodgers lost the game in 16 innings.

Baseball Under the Lights *After 74 years of playing only day games at Wrigley Field, the Chicago Cubs began playing night games in the summer of 1988 (see page 75).*

of the ninth inning. The A's had their ace closer, Dennis Eckersley, on the pitcher's mound, and it looked as if Oakland was going to jump out in front in the Series.

Eckersley walked Mike Davis. Then, as the crowd stood and roared its approval, Gibson, sidelined with a serious knee injury, grabbed a bat and limped up to the plate. It would be his only at-bat in the series, but it was enough. Gibson, wincing in pain, smacked a 3–2 pitch into the right-field seats for a two-run homer that gave the Dodgers the victory and the momentum to take the Series.

Gibson added this dramatic homer to the one he hit four years earlier to help the Detroit Tigers win the 1984 World Series (see page 48). This home run eventually ranked No. 9 in Major League Baseball's Most Memorable Moments campaign in the 2002 season.

NFL Suspends 19 Players

NFL commissioner Pete Rozelle wanted the message to be heard loud and clear: The league would not tolerate drug use, even by its top players. Rozelle announced that 19 NFL players were being suspended for substance abuse.

Among the 19 were defensive superstars Lawrence Taylor of the New York Giants, Dexter Manley of the Washington Redskins, and Bruce Smith of the Buffalo Bills. They were among 18 players who received 30-day suspensions. Tony Collins, a runningback for the Indianapolis Colts, received a one-year suspension.

NFL guidelines state that a player who fails a drug test for the first time receives a warning and treatment. If a player fails a second drug test, he is

1988

suspended for 30 days. A third failure results in a lifetime suspension, although the player may apply for reinstatement based on good behavior.

Oilers Trade Gretzky

Few cities have ever had a love affair with a professional athlete as intense as the relationship between NHL great Wayne Gretzky and the city of Edmonton, Ontario, in Canada. So it was a complete shock when Peter Pocklington, owner of the Edmonton Oilers, announced one of the most startling trades in sports history. Gretzky (along with two other players) had been traded from the Oilers to the Los Angeles Kings (for two players,

three first-round draft choices, and $14.4 million). The details of the trade hardly mattered to Edmonton hockey fans. The Great One (as Gretzky was known) was leaving.

"It's like ripping the heart out of the city," said Edmonton mayor Laurence Decore. Hockey fans in the town agreed. In his nine seasons with the Oilers, Gretzky set 43 NHL scoring records, won eight consecutive Most Valuable Player trophies, captured seven straight scoring titles, and led his team to four Stanley Cup championships. No wonder Canadians felt as if their national treasure had been stolen from them by the United States.

As it turned out, Gretzky himself had requested the trade. In July of 1988, he married American actress Janet Jones. At the time, Canadian hockey fans treated their wedding like a royal affair, tuning in to the event on television and welcoming Jones into their extended "family."

When the trade was announced a month later, though, Canadians blamed Jones for stealing their superstar. Gretzky said Los Angeles offered him a new challenge, to make hockey popular in a city not known for its love of the sport. But he also moved to make it easier for his wife to pursue her acting career.

Gretzky wept openly at the press conference announcing his departure, but Pocklington accused him of acting for the cameras, stating that Gretzky had a huge ego, which is why he requested the trade. The Oilers' owner later refuted the claim, but the damage had been done. The greatest hockey player ever was leaving the country of his birth and the city where he rewrote the NHL record book.

Magnificent Seven *Jackie Joyner-Kersee won the gold medal in the heptathlon—a seven-event competition to identify the world's best female athlete—with a record-setting performance at the Olympics.*

Olympic Sisters-in-Law

After the United States' boycott of the Olympic Games in Moscow in 1980 and the Soviet Union's boycott of the Games in Los Angeles in 1984, the world's two major superpowers finally competed together in the Summer Olympics in the 1988 Games in Seoul, South Korea.

The Soviets dominated these Olympics, winning 132 medals, including 55 gold. But the Americans had numerous memorable performances en route to winning 94 medals, including 36 gold. Chief among them were those by sisters-in-law Jackie Joyner-Kersee and Florence Griffith Joyner.

In some ways, they could not have been more different. Joyner-Kersee was all about hard work, muscle, and sweat, considered by many to be the finest female athlete of the second half of the 20th century. Griffith Joyner (known as "Flo Jo"), also a world-class athlete, combined her great physical abilities with a flashy style and fashion savvy. The two American women teamed up to dominate the track-and-field events in Seoul. They combined to win five gold medals.

Joyner-Kersee broke her own world record in the heptathlon on her way to Olympic gold, shattering the rarely surpassed 7,000-point mark in the event by scoring 7,291 points, almost 400 points ahead of her nearest competitor. (The heptathlon is a seven-event competition made up of the 100-meter hurdles, the shot put, the high jump, the 200-meter race, the long jump, the javelin, and the 800-meter race). She followed up her victory in the heptathlon by setting an Olym-

pic record in the long jump, leaping an amazing 24 feet, 3 1/2 inches to earn her second gold medal. Until Joyner-Kersee did it, no one thought it was possible to win the grueling two-day heptathlon, and then come back and win an individual event. Bruce Jenner, the 1976 Olympic decathlon gold medalist, said of Joyner-Kersee, "She's the greatest multi-sport athlete ever, man or woman."

Flo Jo captured three golds. She won the 100-meter sprint, setting an Olympic record with a time of 10.54 seconds. In the 200-meter race, she set a world record with a time of 21.34 seconds. Her third gold medal came as part of the United States' 400-meter relay team.

The United States also was strong in the swimming and diving events. Seventeen-year-old Janet Evans set a world record on her way to winning the 400-meter freestyle swimming event. She also won gold medals in the 800-meter freestyle and 400-meter individual medley. Matt Biondi won seven swimming medals, including five gold.

Fashion Statements

In addition to her great athletic achievements at the 1988 Summer Olympic Games, Florence Griffith Joyner made some of the most memorable fashion statements of the 1980s.

From her catchy nickname (Flo Jo) to her glittering, sexy track outfits, from colorful, one-legged unitards to outrageous six-inch fingernails and make-up, Flo Jo was style personified. She made no apologies for breaking the rules of how a track star should dress, look, or carry herself.

Flo Jo later went on to design new uniforms for the NBA's Indiana Pacers.

1988

American Greg Louganis (see the box below), arguably the best diver in history, became the first diver to win two gold medals in two consecutive Olympic Games.

In 1984, at the Games in Los Angeles, Louganis won gold in the platform and springboard events. He repeated those victories in Seoul four years later. In 1988, his victory had added drama when Louganis hit his head on the diving board during a preliminary round of the springboard competition, but still came back to win the event.

Johnson Stripped of Gold

In addition to the success of Jackie Joyner-Kersee and Florence Griffith Joyner, the United States picked up another track and field gold medal—although it didn't appear that way at first. Canadian sprinter Ben Johnson defeated his American rival, Carl Lewis, in the 100-meter sprint, running a world record time of 9.79 seconds. Lewis finished second with a time of 9.92. But three days later, Johnson was disqualified and his gold medal was taken away when he tested

Greg Louganis: Secrets and Success

When United States Olympic gold medal diver Greg Louganis hit his head on the diving board during a preliminary round of the springboard competition at the 1988 Olympic Games, it took five stitches to close the wound. Louganis was very upset, not simply because of the injury, but because Louganis was HIV-positive—a fact only a few of his closest friends were aware of.

Had everyone there been aware of Louganis' illness, panic might have ensued. The pool would likely have been drained, the competition disrupted, and the diver himself exposed to scorn or controversy for putting others in potential danger. (In reality, the chlorine in the pool was enough to kill any virus that may have been shed in his blood.)

Louganis recovered from his fall and captured the gold medal in the event the next day, as well as a second gold in platform diving, but the experience shook him deeply. Louganis was gay, something else

only his closest friends knew. He retired from diving after the 1988 games. In 1994 at the Gay Games in New York City, he announced his homosexuality.

Hiding his homosexuality and his disease for years took its toll. "It's been so difficult with the secret, and asking people to keep the secrets," he said in his autobiography, *Breaking the Surface*, published in 1995. "I was feeling like a fake."

In the book he discussed being gay, living with the secret, and living with HIV. His openness led to a greater comfort with himself, and with his place in diving history. "Being gay and being in sports isn't supposed to mix," Louganis said. "I think I proved that wrong."

Three years later, the growing specter of AIDS in American society would find an even more familiar face when Magic Johnson, one of the dominant athletes of the 1980s, announced that he had tested positive for HIV, the virus that causes AIDS.

Other Milestones of 1988

✔ National League president A. Bartlett Giamatti was chosen to become the new baseball commissioner.

✔ Jose Canseco of the Oakland A's became the first player in baseball history to hit 40 homers and steal 40 bases in the same season.

✔ The Miami Heat and the Charlotte Hornets joined the NBA.

✔ The catcher's helmet was required in the major leagues for the first time.

✔ The first African-American referee in the NFL, Johnny Grier, made his debut.

✔ Nike's "Just Do It" ad campaign debuted, encouraging everyone to go for their dreams, emulate their sports heroes, and, of course, buy Nike shoes. The phrase quickly became a part of American popular culture.

Jose Canseco

positive for ozolol, an anabolic steroid that was banned by the International Olympic Committee. Johnson was barred from competing on Canada's national team for life and was sent home in disgrace. The gold medal was given to Lewis, who had won four gold medals at the Games in 1984 (see page 48).

Johnson's fall from grace led to increased efforts to eliminate the use of performance-enhancing drugs in the Olympics. More rigorous testing was introduced. Not only were athletes tested immediately after competitions, but also, in some countries, random tests were performed throughout athletes' training periods.

Big-Screen Baseball

Two of the best baseball movies of all time were released in 1988. *Bull Durham*, starring Kevin Costner, Susan Sarandon, and Tim Robbins, was written and directed by Ron Shelton, a former minor-league baseball player. It tells the story of a career minor-league catcher who is asked to whip an up-and-coming pitcher into shape and to teach him the ways of the game.

Eight Men Out, directed by John Sayles, based on the book by Eliot Asinof, tells the story of the 1919 Black Sox scandal, which almost destroyed baseball. John Cusack played Buck Weaver, D.B. Sweeney played "Shoeless" Joe Jackson, and Sayles played writer Ring Lardner. The heavily favored 1919 Chicago White Sox lost the World Series that year, and subsequently were accused of being paid by gamblers to purposely lose. It led to player suspensions and to the appointment of the first baseball commissioner, Judge Kenesaw Mountain Landis, to rid the game of gambling's influence—which was considerable at the time.

1989

On the Air

S By the end of the 1980s, the influence of television on sports in America was so strong that it had direct effects on the very structure of the games. Teams moved to new cities because the television markets were larger. Television revenue had become more important than the money collected from fans paying to get into the actual event. Filling the home stadium became less important than local television deals, which more than made up for empty seats.

Entire leagues were restructured and additional tiers of postseason games were added because they made for good television. People who might not follow a particular sport every day throughout the regular season did show an interest in the playoffs. So television gave them more playoff games, which, of course, meant more advertising revenue—charged at much higher rates than during the regular season.

The big television money led to even bigger sponsorship agreements and huge contracts, with dollars reaching into the previously inconceivable millions, for America's professional athletes.

Television's marriage with sports had humble beginnings. The first television broadcast of a Major League Baseball game was on August 26, 1939, when WSBX-TV aired the action between the Brooklyn Dodgers and the Cincinnati Reds at Ebbets Field in Brooklyn, New York. It was seen by a few hundred people watching the approximately 400 television sets in all of New York City. The Dodgers and Reds split a doubleheader that day.

By the 1950s, sports were a staple of television programming in the still relatively young medium. Friday night boxing matches and Saturday afternoon baseball games became regular parts of the lives of sports-loving Americans.

The 1960s saw big television money just starting to make its way into professional sports. The man most responsible for this was NFL commissioner Pete Rozelle, who brought his league into the television spotlight and into the hearts and living rooms of American sports fans. It was television in the 1960s that catapulted football ahead of baseball—the traditional American national pastime—as the most popular professional team sport in the country.

Joe Cool *Joe Montana helped make the San Francisco 49ers the NFL's team of the decade. He led his team to the winning score late in Super Bowl XXIII (see page 84).*

Rozelle's television contracts in the 1960s brought big money into the league. When CBS began televising NFL games in 1956, the network negotiated a separate contract with each of the 12 teams in the league. Each team got between $35,000 and $185,000 directly from the network for the rights to broadcast its games. In

1989

1962, Rozelle worked out a package deal in which CBS paid the league $4.5 million dollars over two years for the rights to broadcast the games of all the teams.

In 1970, the television networks paid $50 million to broadcast NFL games. In 1985 that figure rose to $450 million. As the 1980s ended, the NFL signed four-year deals with CBS, ABC, ESPN, and Turner Broadcasting for a total of $3.6 billion. In the years between those early deals and the multi-billion-dollar contracts, the NFL expanded from 12 teams to 14, then 16, and finally 28.

In 1950, Major League Baseball signed a deal with the Gillette razor company for $6 million for the rights to the World Series and All-Star Games over a six-year period. Under the terms of the deal, Gillette ads would run exclusively on all television and radio broadcasts of the games. In 1970, the television networks paid $18 million for the rights to broadcast baseball, and in 1985 that amount had grown to $160 million. In 1989, baseball signed a deal with CBS for $1.1 billion, and another deal with ESPN for $400 million.

The huge, ever-expanding flow of money into the pockets of team owners and the leagues did not go unnoticed by the players. They began to demand their fair share of the revenue. Unions were formed, strikes were staged, and restrictive legal clauses binding players to teams for life were challenged and overturned in court. This led to free agency and bidding wars between teams, each club hoping to secure the top players by offering more than the competition. In the end, the players were big winners, commanding sala-

ries unthinkable a few years earlier.

As the 1980s drew to a close, sports and television were as inseparable as a catcher and his face mask. Sports has always been a business, but with big television money leading to huge influence, the realization that in modern sports the bottom line was often of greater interest than the final score became an accepted reality.

Dramatic Super Bowl

With a little more than three minutes remaining in the game and his San Francisco 49ers trailing the Cincinnati Bengals by three points in Super Bowl XXIII in Miami on January 22, quarterback Joe Montana entered the huddle. His team was 92 yards from the most dramatic Super Bowl victory to date, but it could have been a touch-football game in the park for the man they called "Joe Cool."

"Hey, Harris, check it out—there's John Candy," Montana told young offensive lineman Harris Barton, pointing to the actor-comedian in the stands. Barton had been fidgeting nervously during a television time out, but Montana's message was clear: Nothing to worry about.

Cincinnati had forged its lead largely behind a tough defense and a 93-yard, third-quarter kickoff return by Stanford Jennings. San Francisco tied the score early in the fourth quarter on a 14-yard touchdown pass from Montana to his favorite receiver, Jerry Rice, but Cincinnati regained the advantage on a 40-yard field goal by Jim Breech. And so the 49ers trailed 16–13 with three minutes and 10 seconds on the clock and the ball on their own eight-yard line. It was time for Montana, one of the greatest quarterbacks in NFL history at working under pressure, to take things into his experienced hands.

Mixing pass plays and running plays, Montana launched the touchdown drive that gave the 49ers a 20–16 victory. The winning points came on his 10-yard touchdown pass to John Taylor with 34 seconds left.

Montana finished with a Super Bowl-record (since broken) 357 passing yards, although Rice was named the game's MVP for catching 11 passes for 215 yards.

The victory was San Francisco's third (of four) in the Super Bowl in the 1980s, and it came in Bill Walsh's final game as the 49ers' head coach. Walsh (1931–2007) remains the only man to win a Super Bowl in his final game on the sidelines.

Lemieux Passes Gretzky

For the decade of the 1980s, any talk about the NHL naturally centered around Wayne Gretzky. Fans of hockey in the '80s were lucky enough to have watched the sport as its greatest player dominated the league.

As the decade drew to a close, however, a new star emerged. Twenty-three-year-old Mario Lemieux of the Pittsburgh Penguins won the NHL scoring title, finishing ahead of Gretzky for the second consecutive year. Lemieux, a 6-foot-4, 200-pound native of Montreal, Quebec, scored 85 goals and handed out 114 assists for a total of 199 points—the most ever achieved by anyone other than Gretzky.

Along the way, Lemieux established himself as the league's best player.

Cool Under Pressure

Sometimes all it takes is being told that you're not good enough. Joe Montana was not highly touted heading into the 1979 NFL draft. All he had done in college was work his way up from seventh-string quarterback for the University of Notre Dame to starter, lead the team in staging amazing late-game comebacks, and take the squad to the national championship in 1977.

But he never looked that good on paper. He was too skinny, he couldn't throw the ball all that far, and even his short passes looked a bit wobbly. He didn't have the sculpted body or rocket-launcher arm that seemed to be a requirement for modern quarterbacks. He was more of a throwback to the days of Johnny Unitas, Len Dawson, and Bart Starr, all of whom played in the 1950s.

The San Francisco 49ers picked Montana in the third round of the 1979 draft. By his third year as a pro, he had become the 49ers' full-time starting quarterback. That season, he led San Francisco to a last-minute, come-from-behind victory against the Dallas Cowboys, the team that had dominated the NFL in the 1970s, in the NFC Championship Game (see page 26). He then won the first of his four Super Bowls.

There has never been anyone cooler under pressure. If there was time on the clock and Montana had the ball, the 49ers always had a chance.

1989

Larger and stronger than Gretzky, Lemieux racked up nine hat tricks (scoring three goals in one game) in 1988–89 and set an NHL record by scoring 13 short-handed goals (when your team is short a player because of a penalty). Pittsburgh scored a record 118 power-play goals (when you team has one more player than the opposition because of a penalty), and Lemieux was involved in 109 of those. His 199 points is the fourth-highest total in NHL history.

Giamatti Bans Pete Rose

A. Bartlett Giamatti, former president of the National League, became baseball commissioner on April 1. A lifelong fan, devoted to baseball's traditions, Giamatti earned his reputation for being tough in dealing with unions as president of Yale University.

Giamatti spent most of his first five months as commissioner leading an investigation into the gambling activities of Pete Rose. Rose is baseball's all-time hits leader and was one of the game's best players for more than 20 years.

As a result of the investigation, a huge amount of evidence surfaced, chronicling years of gambling by Rose, including the devastating revelation that he had bet on baseball games. On August 24, Giamatti announced that an agreement had been reached banning Rose from any further involvement with the game of baseball.

Rose signed the agreement, which stated that he accepted the punishment without admitting nor denying his guilt. Rose was also allowed to apply for reinstatement into the game after a year, but

Giamatti would give no guarantee that his position would change at that time.

This painful banishment immediately asserted Giamatti's power as commissioner, though it brought him no joy. Rose would have been a certain selection for baseball's Hall of Fame based on his performance as a player, and to this day he remains out of the Hall and banned from the game.

This sad series of events was immediately followed by a shocking tragedy that stunned the baseball world. On September 1, Giamatti died suddenly of a heart attack while at his summer cottage in Massachusetts—eight days after banning Rose from baseball. Giamatti was just 51 years old.

Earthquake Rocks Series

On October 17, more than 60,000 fans packed Candlestick Park in San Francisco for game three of the World Series between the Giants and their cross-bay rivals, the Oakland Athletics. The Athletics had won the first two games handily, but the Giants' fans on hand were anxious to see the first World Series game at Candlestick in 27 years.

In a flash, though, all concerns about the Giants getting back into the Series were forgotten: At 5:04 P.M., with pre-game ceremonies just getting started, a 6.9-magnitude earthquake rocked the San Francisco Bay Area, knocking out power and causing widespread destruction.

Players and fans remained amazingly calm despite swaying press boxes and a sudden loss of power. Live television and radio broadcasts were temporarily knocked off the air. The ballpark had some damage, but mostly held up to the stress, and no one inside was hurt.

Players scrambled to find their families. When broadcasts were restored, viewers who had tuned in for the game saw players holding their children and hugging their wives, all thoughts of a ball game replaced by concern for the safety of loved ones. Anxious fans in the ballpark waited for word of what to do next.

Baseball commissioner Fay Vincent, who had been in the job just a little more than a month, reacted quickly. He postponed the game and began emptying the ballpark before darkness set in.

As fans left the stadium, they had no idea of the extent of the devastation in the surrounding area. When the earthquake ended, 67 people were dead, and roads, bridges, and buildings had collapsed, causing billions of dollars of damage.

Suddenly, the all-Bay-Area World Series had lost its urgency, as people faced the more urgent tasks of rebuilding their city and their lives. Repairs were made to the stadium, and, although some called for the rest of the World Series to be cancelled, Vincent and San Francisco mayor Art Agnos eventually decided to resume the Series beginning October 27. The A's went on to complete their four-game sweep, although the games and final scores all seemed anticlimactic.

San Francisco Giants centerfielder Brett Butler put it best. "At the start, I realized what a privilege it was to be in the Series. Now, I realize what a privilege it is to be alive. When people think of the 1989 Series, they're not going to remember who won, but who survived."

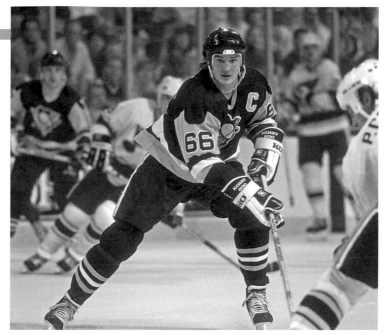

As Good as the Great One? *By the end of the decade, Mario Lemieux may have surpassed Wayne Gretzky as hockey's best player (see page 85).*

Shell Breaks Color Barrier

Art Shell took over as head coach of the Los Angeles Raiders on October 3. He became the NFL's first African-American head coach in 64 years.

Before Shell, the last African-American to coach an NFL team was Fritz Pollard of the Hammond (Indiana) Pros. From 1923 to 1925, Pollard, a running back, was the Pros' player-coach.

Shell was a star tackle in his playing days who was one of the pillars, along with guard Gene Upshaw, of the Oakland Raiders' offensive line in the 1970s. Shell played in 207 regular-season games from 1968 to 1982 and earned eight Pro Bowl selections. He was inducted into the Pro Football Hall of Fame shortly before the start of the 1989 season.

1989

After the Raiders stumbled to a 1–3 start that year, owner Al Davis turned to Shell, who was coaching the offensive line, to succeed young Mike Shanahan as head coach. Under Shell's leadership, the Raiders won seven of their next 10 games, although they failed to make the playoffs. (The next season, however, Shell's team went 12–4 and reached the AFC title game.)

Shell coached the Raiders through 1994, and compiled a 56–41 record (including postseason). He took his team to the playoffs three times. He returned to coach the Raiders in 2006, but did not have the same success, winning only two games in a one-season stint.

Shell's appointment paved the way for other African-American head coaches in the NFL. In 2009, six league teams began the season with African-Americans at the helm, and a seventh black head coach was hired during the season.

Still, the first African-American to coach in the NFL's modern era was a long time coming. By contrast, the NBA hired its first black head coach in 1966, when future Hall-of-Famer Bill Russell became player-coach of the Boston Celtics. Between 1966 and 1989, when Shell broke the NFL coaching color barrier, the NBA had 18 black head coaches.

The first black Major League Baseball manager was hired in 1975, when Hall-of-Famer Frank Robinson became manager of the Cleveland Indians. Between that year and 1989, baseball had four black managers. Hispanics have also made major in-roads in managerial positions since then.

Two Times Ninety

Almost from the moment that wide receiver Jerry Rice joined the San Francisco 49ers as a first-round draft choice in 1985, he dominated headlines with his remarkable play-making ability. During the 49ers' nationally televised 30–27 victory over the Los Angeles Rams on December 11 in Anaheim, however, the incomparable Rice took a back seat to John Taylor. That Monday night, San Francisco's No. 2 wideout became the first NFL player to score two touchdowns of more than 90 yards in the same game.

Taylor turned short passes from Joe Montana into touchdowns of 92 yards and 95 yards. He helped the 49ers rally from a 17-point deficit to beat their NFC West rivals.

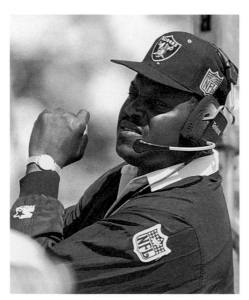

Coaching Pioneer *The Los Angeles Raiders made Art Shell the NFL's first African-American head coach in 64 years.*

Other Milestones of 1989

✔ Bill White was named president of baseball's National League. He became the first African-American to preside over a major sports league in United States history.

✔ Kareem Abdul-Jabbar retired from the NBA as its career leader in points (38,387), games (1,560), and minutes played (56,446).

✔ Greg LeMond won his second Tour de France bicycle race in July.

✔ Jim Abbott, a baseball pitcher with only one hand, played in the major leagues. Abbott went 12-12 for the California Angels.

✔ Texas Rangers pitcher Nolan Ryan fanned the 5,000th batter of his career on August 22.

Jim Abbott

✔ Triple Crown winner Secretariat, considered by many to be the greatest thoroughbred race horse of all time, died on October 4.

✔ On October 25, Los Angeles Kings star Wayne Gretzky passed Gordie Howe as the NHL's all-time leading scorer (1,852 points). Gretzky set the mark in Edmonton against the Oilers, the team for whom he had his greatest years.

✔ The International Amateur Basketball Federation opened the Olympics to all professional athletes, including those from the NBA.

✔ Chris Evert became the first tennis player, male or female, to win 1,000 career singles matches.

San Francisco, playing under new head coach George Seifert (Bill Walsh's successor), won 14 games during the 1989 regular season to beat out the Rams for the division title. The two teams met again in the NFC Championship Game that year, but that game wasn't so close: San Francisco won in a rout, 30–3.

The 49ers then went on to win their second consecutive Super Bowl by blasting the Denver Broncos 55–24 in game XXIV on January 28, 1990, at the Superdome in New Orleans. Seifert became just the second rookie coach (after the Colts' Don McCafferty in 1970) to win the Super Bowl.

RESOURCES

1980s Events and Personalities

Boycott: Stolen Dreams of the 1980 Moscow Olympic Games
By Tom Caraccioli and Jerry Caraccioli (New York: New Chapter Press, 2008)
This book profiles 18 athletes who were denied the chance to compete in the 1980 Summer Olympics because of the United States' boycott of the Games, and looks at the events leading up to that decision.

The Boys of Winter: The Untold Story of a Coach, a Dream, and the 1980 U.S. Olympic Hockey Team
By Wayne Coffey (New York: Crown Publishers, 2005)
The author details how American coach Herb Brooks molded a group of college kids and minor-league players into the team beat the vaunted Soviet squad in a memorable upset in the 1980 Winter Olympic Games.

The 1980s (American Popular Culture Through History)
By Bob Batchelor and Scott Stoddart (Westport, Connecticut: Greenwood Press, 2006).
Check out what life was like in America in the 1980s, from youth issues to advertising, fashion, music, and lots more.

We Were Champions: The 49ers' Dynasty in Their Own Words
By Phil Barber (Chicago: Triumph Books, 2002)
San Francisco built the team of the eighties in the National Football League, winning four Super Bowls and featuring such legendary players as quarterback Joe Montana and wide receiver Jerry Rice.

American Sports History

The Complete Book of the Olympics
By David Wallechinsky and Jaime Loucky (London: Aurum Press, 2008)
An extremely detailed look at every Winter and Summer Olympics from 1896 to the present, including complete lists of medal winners and short biographies of important American and international athletes.

The Encyclopedia of North American Sports History, Second Edition
By Ralph Hickok (New York: Facts on File, 2002)
This title includes articles on the origins of all the major sports as well as capsule biographies of key figures.

Encyclopedia of Women and Sport in America
Edited by Carol Oglesby et al. (Phoenix: Oryx Press, 1998)
A large overview of not only key female personalities on and off the playing field, but a look at issues surrounding women and sports.

Encyclopedia of World Sport
Edited by David Levinson and Karen Christensen (New York: Oxford University Press, 1999)
This wide-ranging book contains short articles on an enormous variety of sports, personalities, events, and issues, most of which have some connection to American sports history. This is a great starting point for additional research.

The ESPN Baseball Encyclopedia
Edited by Gary Gillette and Pete Palmer (New York: Sterling, 2008, fifth edition)
This is the latest version of a long-running baseball record and stats books, including the career totals of every Major Leaguer. Essays in the book cover baseball history, team history, overviews of baseball in other countries, and articles about the role of women and minorities in the game.

ESPN SportsCentury
Edited by Michael McCambridge (New York: Hyperion, 1999)
Created to commemorate the 20th century in sports, this book features essays by well known sportswriters as well as commentary by popular ESPN broadcasters. Each decade's chapter features an in-depth story about the key event of that time period.

NFL Record & Fact Book
Edited by Jon Zimmer, Randall Liu, and Matt Marini (New York: Time Inc. Home Entertainment, 2009)
An indispensable reference source for NFL fans and media personnel.

The Sporting News Chronicle of 20th Century Sports
By Ron Smith (New York: BDD/Mallard Press, 1992)
A good single-volume history of key sports events. They are presented as if written right after the event, thus giving the text a "you are there" feel.

Sports of the Times
By David Fischer and William Taafe. (New York: Times Books, 2003)
A unique format tracks the top sports events on each day of the calendar year. Find out the biggest event for every day from January 1 to December 31.

Sports History Web Sites

ESPN.com
www.sports.espn.go.com
The Web site run by the national cable sports channel contains numerous history sections within each sport. This one for baseball is the largest and includes constantly updated statistics on baseball.

Official League Web Sites
www.nfl.com
www.nba.com
www.mlb.com
www.nhl.com
Each of the major sports leagues has history sections on their official Web sites.

Official Olympics Web Site
http://www.olympic.org/uk/games/index_uk.asp
Complete history of the Olympic Games, presented by the International Olympic Committee.

The Sports Illustrated Vault
http://sportsillustrated.cnn.com/vault/
Since its first issue in 1954, Sports Illustrated *has been a must-read for fans everywhere. You can go down memory lane in this trove of features, photos, and covers from the magazine.*

Sports Reference
www.sports-reference.com
By far the most detailed central site, including separate sections on baseball, basketball, football, hockey, and the Olympics. The sections include player stats, team histories, records from all seasons past, and much more.

INDEX